# Training the City Dog

# What people are saying about Training The City Dog

*"...many of the [tips] aren't covered in any dog training book I've ever read."*

*"...I had a great weekend with Gibson...a timid country dog who turned into a sophisticated, hip city dog while he was here...I know it was a successful weekend in part because I had read your book!"*

*"A very comprehensive guide for caring for and raising your dog in an urban setting. Gives great suggestions for all kinds of situations."*

*"Comprehensive and lighthearted."*

*"Great information!"*

*"Great advice!"*

# Training The City Dog

## Tips For
### High-rise Housebreaking
### Banishing Barking
### Critical Commands
### Proper Petiquette
### And Uniquely Urban Situations

## Katherine Kane

City Pet Books, Milwaukee

TRAINING THE CITY DOG: Tips For High-rise Housebreaking, Banishing Barking, Critical Commands, Proper Petiquette, And Uniquely Urban Situations

Copyright © 2009 Katherine Kane

Published by City Pet Books, LLC, Milwaukee

All rights reserved. No part of this book may be used, reproduced or transmitted in any form without the written permission of City Pet Books, except for brief quotations in critical articles and reviews.

Sketches by Jean Kane
Cover design by Pamela Stoesser
Edited and indexed by Linda Presto

ISBN 978-0-9828906-0-8
Library of Congress Control Number: 2010911072
1. Dog–Training  2. Dog–Behavior  3. Puppies–Training
4. Puppies–Behavior  5. Animal Training  6. Dog Owners
7. Puppies–Training–Handbooks, manuals, etc.

This book is presented with the intent to provide accurate information regarding the subject matter. Although every reasonable precaution has been taken in the preparation of this book, the author expressly disclaims responsibility for errors, omissions, or adverse effects arising from use of the information contained herein. The information contained herein is to be used at the reader's discretion. It is not to be considered a substitute for professional legal advice, professional training, and/or veterinary care.

*Dedicated To*

*City Dogs Everywhere*

# Contents

| | |
|---|---:|
| **About This Book** | **15** |
| **Eight Tips ~ High-rise Housebreaking And Related Matters** | **19** |
| 1  The Fear Factor | 19 |
| 2  Cue Words | 22 |
| 3  Bell Ringing | 24 |
| 4  Keys! | 26 |
| 5  Carpets | 27 |
| 6  Clean Up | 28 |
| 7  Resources | 30 |
| 8  Treats | 30 |
| **Eight Tips ~ People** | **32** |
| 1  Dog Dislikers | 32 |
| 2  Only My Dog | 33 |
| 3  Dog Lovers – Without Dogs | 33 |

| 4 Pickled People | 34 |
|---|---|
| 5 People In Uniforms | 35 |
| 6 Perfect People | 36 |
| 7 Children | 37 |
| 8 Treats | 38 |

**Seven Tips ~ Dogs, Cats, And Other Urban Critters** — 39

| 1 Monster Dog | 39 |
|---|---|
| 2 Overly Friendly Dogs | 41 |
| 3 Guide Dogs And Service Dogs | 42 |
| 4 Horses | 43 |
| 5 Chipmunks, Squirrels, Geese | 44 |
| 6 Other Non-Dogs | 45 |
| 7 Treats | 47 |

**Six Tips ~ Absolutely Critical Commands And Related Topics** — 48

| 1 Leave It! | 51 |
|---|---|
| 2 Drop It! | 54 |
| 3 Heel! | 57 |
| 4 Come! And Down & Stay! On Command | 62 |

| | | |
|---|---|---|
| 5 | Collars And Leashes | 64 |
| 6 | Treats And Play | 66 |

**Five Tips ~ Sidewalk Cafes, Stores, Flowers, And Vehicles** — 67

| | | |
|---|---|---|
| 1 | Sidewalk Cafes | 67 |
| 2 | Stores And Other Small Businesses | 68 |
| 3 | Flowers And Plants | 69 |
| 4 | Vehicles | 70 |
| 5 | Treats | 73 |

**Seven Tips ~ Tags, Licenses, And Health And Legal Whatnot** — 74

| | | |
|---|---|---|
| 1 | Dog License | 75 |
| 2 | Leash Laws | 75 |
| 3 | Shots And Preventive Medications | 80 |
| 4 | Dog Boots | 81 |
| 5 | Nipping And Biting | 83 |
| 6 | Tied To The Bicycle Rack And All Alone | 85 |
| 7 | Treats | 87 |

**Eight Tips ~ Barking** — 88

| | | |
|---|---|---|
| 1 | Barking Breeds | 88 |

Table of Contents

| | | |
|---|---|---|
| 2 | Learned Barking | 89 |
| 3 | Rewarded Barking | 89 |
| 4 | Rewarded Silence | 90 |
| 5 | Home Alone Barking | 90 |
| 6 | Normal Barking | 94 |
| 7 | Two More Tips | 95 |
| 8 | Resources | 96 |

**Eleven Tips ~ Miscellaneous This And That** — 97

| | | |
|---|---|---|
| 1 | Treats | 97 |
| 2 | Lost Dogs | 98 |
| 3 | Wet Dog | 101 |
| 4 | Elevators | 102 |
| 5 | Crates | 104 |
| 6 | Fireworks | 105 |
| 7 | Fire Alarms | 105 |
| 8 | Wheelchairs | 108 |
| 9 | Outdoor Events | 108 |
| 10 | My Dog Is Friendly | 110 |

| 11 Walking More Than One Dog | 111 |
|---|---|
| **Some Last Words** | **112** |
| 1  Training | 112 |
| 2  Dogs In The City | 113 |
| 3  Take-Aways | 114 |
| 4  Have Fun | 116 |
| **Index** | **117** |

## About This Book

*Training The City Dog* offers training tips for city dog owners and is a survival guide for city dogs. It outlines city challenges and offers suggestions for handling them:

- Housebreaking that works for high-rise reality
- Skills for dealing with city people and city animals
- Commands every city dog should know
- Health and legal matters
- Special city situations and city petiquette

The inspiration for this book came during the process of training a puppy for life in a city high-rise. I searched everywhere for information that offered me some perspective on living with a dog in a city. There is a lot of information out there about training puppies, but not much specific and detailed help with training puppies to be good city citizens. And there is even less information about how to help your older dog adapt to a move into the city.

It has been five years since the trial-by-fire adventure with my puppy. During her early days and over the five years since, I gathered what information I could from books and online resources. I talked with dog trainers, dog groomers, doggie day care owners, dog walkers, pet store owners, and other dog professionals. I talked with people who wished there were no dogs in cities in order to learn why they felt that way and what might make them change their minds. I talked with apartment owners and condo board members to learn what drove them crazy about having dogs in their buildings and about why some decided banish dogs entirely. I talked with and observed many city dog owners. Everything I learned from these sources, together with my own experience, is the foundation for this book. Added to this is feedback I have received from readers of *The City Dog: Dog Training Tips For City Living* iPhone App, an abridged edition of this book.

Even though some of them sound quite unbelievable, the situations described in this book are real, not imaginary. They are situations I personally witnessed, learned about in conversations with others about dogs in the city, or both. Names have been changed to protect the innocent (and the guilty).

I have not attempted to make this book a comprehensive puppy training book, although I have included specific training steps for some of the critical commands. This is meant to be a companion volume to the comprehensive dog training book of your choice and a supplement to online references. It is designed to fill the gaps between what standard resources offer and the reality of urban life with your dog.

I encourage you to take your best furry friend to training class, no matter what its age. Puppy training is not only unbelievably helpful, it is also loads of fun for both you and your puppy. Obedience training, sometimes called "good manners" class, picks up where puppy classes end and takes you and your dog to another level. Dogs of any age can benefit from "good manners" class, and you can attend more than once. If you are moving your suburban or country dog to the city, class is a good way to socialize your dog with a lot of other dogs and refresh skills you may not have used for many years. Classes are a great refresher when your dog reaches a new stage of development. Most training classes my dog and I attend are composed of a mix of newbies and repeats. A lot of us who own dogs that tend to be sassy find that repeating the classes every few years helps us and our dogs remember who is supposed to be in charge. It also brings us up to date on new training techniques, dog diet research, and new collar technologies.

If there are tricks classes in your area, don't pass up the opportunity. They are fun for dogs and people of all ages. Whoever said that you can't teach an old dog new tricks wasn't fully informed. In one of the tricks classes my dog and I attended, the class star was a nine-year-old adopted mix. He was the first to raise his paw whenever a question was asked, was always chosen to come to the front to show the rest of us how to do something, and was consistently perfect on all tests. Tricks class will give you and your dog lots of new games to play and ways to impress your friends and family. (And on the practical side, if you inadvertently leave a light on at night, you don't have to get out of bed to turn it off; your dog can do it for you.)

Throughout the book, I refer to dogs by name because it is so tedious to constantly write "your dog" or "the dog" or "a dog." The names were randomly selected. As they say, any similarity to an actual dog of that particular name is purely coincidental. Sometimes I use feminine pronouns; other times I use masculine pronouns. I tried for equitable distribution.

I have not provided links to Internet sites in my references because one never knows when one site will disappear and a great new site will appear. Instead, I have provided key words for you to search.

With all this introductory stuff said, let's get down to the nitty-gritty of living with a dog in a city amid a multitude of sights, smells, sounds, people, dogs, and other urban critters.

## ~ Eight Tips ~
## High-rise Housebreaking And Related Matters

Let's start with one of the biggest challenges—calls of nature. As you go through this period, try to keep in mind that this is just a fraction of the lifetime you will spend with your dog. You'll get through it, so don't be discouraged. This chapter has a few tips on housebreaking, to supplement what you learn from your puppy training resources and in your training class. The rest of the chapter is devoted to related matters.

So you have this adorable little bundle of fur and fun. Or you have a dog that is accustomed to going in and out between the house and a yard. Now you live way above ground level. There is a long hallway, a slow elevator, an expansive lobby, a crowded sidewalk, and a busy street between where you are and where you need to be in thirty seconds or less.

### 1  The Fear Factor

When you take your dog out for his first few walks in the city, it can be a very scary experience. The little guy may be only a few inches tall, if he's a puppy.

Or he may be the size of a horse and several years old. But there he is amid belching busses, screaming sirens, honking cars, yelling people, and feet and legs scurrying past. Remember, you are starting the housebreaking routine, but your friend is making a big transition. If he is a puppy, he is accustomed to being in a snuggly place where his companions have four legs and are about his size. If he's a full-grown suburban or country dog, he is coming from much calmer territory with familiar smells and sounds.

Try to have Charley's first few trips out happen at times when things are relatively quiet—very early morning, late evening, Sunday. That is not always practical, but it's best if possible. For his first few forays into the big city world, take him to the nearest place of relative calm and spend some quiet time with him next to you. Watch and listen to all that is going on. Make it quality together time instead of stressed "hurry up" time. Through it all, you must be absolutely calm and collected. All this chaos is normal for you; when you communicate that to Charley, soon it will be normal for him, too.

If you are moving Charley into the city from a suburban or country place, try to visit a city for walks as often as possible before the move. Any city will familiarize him with noise and activity. It will also give you an idea of what to expect. If he is frightened and stressed, even after some repeat trips into a city, talk with your vet about possible solutions. The farther ahead you can prepare, the better.

You will read about or hear housebreaking rules from non-city dog trainers that will not be easy to follow in a city. One of these is that you *must* take your dog to a place that has no distractions. Well, that won't be possible in the middle of a city. But not to worry. You *can* housebreak your dog in the middle of chaos. Take your dog to the nearest available and appropriate spot.

Another piece of suburban advice that doesn't always translate well to city life is that you should take your dog to the same place every time. That might be possible. If so, then go ahead and do that. But know that you can housebreak your puppy without having to return to the same spot each time.

I'm not saying these bits of advice won't make things easier. What I am saying is that your dog is smart. Doing nature's business comes naturally. There are millions of housebroken dogs in cities throughout the world. Your dog can be one of them.

A bit of advice from some trainers is that you should not "paper train" your puppy. Some trainers are adamant that this is a very bad way to go. However, paper training is just plain common sense for middle-of-the-night and first-thing-in-the-morning city puppy needs. Going outside with a puppy at 3:00 in the morning is not always a wise thing to do in a city. First thing in the morning, your pup is not likely to wait patiently while you get up and put some clothes on. So go ahead. Line the bathtub or shower stall with newspaper and go with paper training at those times of the day when it makes sense. Take your pup outside at those times of day when that makes sense.

Paper training is also sometimes advised as a transition for people who will be using a litter box for their dog (although some sources advise starting with the litter box right off the bat). You might be thinking I have gone batty, but there really are litter boxes especially for dogs. And dog litter, too. Amazing! If Tiddly Winks is a small dog, you may want to seriously consider the litter box route. Litter box training for an older dog that is moving into a city may be a larger challenge than starting with a puppy, but it can be done. If you live in the snowbelt, you can be smug as you watch all those owners of huge dogs trundling outside in the elements several times a day. [Web search "dog litter box training" for more information.]

## 2  Cue Words

Distractions are everywhere. You sprained your ankle and have a severe case of funny-bone from banging your elbow on the door to successfully get Homer to the right spot without accident. Leaves are skittering, children are romping, a puppy is trundling up the sidewalk toward you, and the sweet man from the deli wants to chat with Homer. (Imagine how good he smells to dogs.) You are freezing because it's November and your coat and gloves are nowhere near your body. Homer is having the time of his life—so much to watch, so much to chase, so much to smell. No matter that you risk frostbite, don't you dare go inside until Homer has a memory flash and does his business. Just remind yourself that this is better than cleaning a double mess off the carpet inside. In no time, Homer will learn that going outside attached to a leash means that he *must* do his job.

If Homer is a puppy, he probably will not have come with a cue word for taking care of business. Start teaching him a cue word right away. Any word or phrase you will use consistently will work. *Hurry up!* is a good one, because that's what you'll be thinking most of the time.

This is really very simple. The instant Homer starts to do his business, you say *Hurry up!* (or whatever words you decide to use). Every single time. When he is finished, tell him he was a good dog to *Hurry up!* and give him a treat. If you say the same thing over and over again, it won't take long for Homer to associate the words with the act, especially if he gets excellent rewards for doing what you have asked (even though he would have done it anyway).

Obviously if Homer doesn't need to go, no amount of saying *Hurry up!* will make him go. But in time, you will have a good idea of when he needs to go. If you take him out at these times, and when he lets you know he needs to go, the cue word will focus his attention on doing his business. Distractions are so much fun—for Homer, not for you. The purpose of the cue word is to keep Homer from becoming distracted and remind him that he is outside for a reason.

If Homer is used to romping around in a back yard and doing his business whenever, teach him his cue word before you move. In addition to teaching suburban Homer a cue word, you should also accustom him to being walked outside on a leash to do his job. This will be good training for both of you, since you probably open that door for Homer's exit and entry, and then do your own thing in between. [Web search "housebreaking cue word" for more tips.]

## 3  Bell Ringing

If litter box training isn't the best approach for you and your dog, train your dog to be a bell ringer. Hang a bell on the door handle. Attractive bells are readily available during the winter holidays. The bird section of pet stores also has bells on ribbons and Velcro bands.

If you are going to get a puppy, hang a bell on the door handle before you bring the puppy home for the first time. From the very minute Moppet arrives, she will associate the sound of a bell with the opening of the door. Before long, she will associate the opening of the door with a trip outside. How wonderful is that! Pretty soon Moppet will be ringing the bell to let you know you should open the door and take her out.

If you already have Moppet and you haven't moved yet, hang the bell on the door you usually use to take her out so she can start associating the sound of the bell with the opening of the door. She may surprise you by learning to ring the bell even before you move. When you first bring Moppet to her new home in the city, make sure the same bell is hanging on the door to exit your living space. This helps her learn which door is the inside-outside door. Yes, Moppet will be confused at first because in her former home she only had one door between inside and outside. In a high-rise there will be several doors between inside and outside, but only one door that starts the trek outside. She will learn that this is her inside-outside door.

If you are already in your city home, get a bell and hang it on the door handle. Moppet will figure it out. They are smart, these dogs.

It will take a while for Moppet to learn how much time is needed between the ringing of the bell and the act itself. If she has always gone through one door to get outside, give her a *huge* break. She must learn a completely new routine and there may be accidents. Remember, now she is learning that she must take a hike to get outside—down hallways, maybe stairs, maybe an elevator ride, probably through several doors.

Whether Moppet is a brand new puppy or just new to city life, she will probably give you only a second or two of warning at first. The bell will ring and you will have time to make a mad dash for the nearest magic spot. Don't forget little Moppet in your hurry to get outside! No kidding—that happens to even the smartest of urban dog owners.

The day *will* come when Moppet gives you enough advance notice, allowing you time to put on boots, scarf, hat, coat, and mittens. If you live in a warm part of the world—lucky you! This will be much easier.

No matter how annoying it is, during the training process, take her out every time she rings the bell. Naturally Moppet is no dummy; she will probably ring the bell when she wants to go out to play. You can sort that out later when she gets this housebreaking thing down perfectly. You will begin to understand when she needs to go out relative to when she last ate or had water. But at first, take her out every single time she rings the bell. Give her tons of delighted praise if she seriously needed to go outside. If it is a false alarm, save commenting on how you really feel for when she can't hear you.

The fact that some dogs will take advantage of this nifty trick and ring the bell all the time is the reason some trainers think bell ringing is not a good training technique. If this is also your opinion, feel free to ignore this tip. However, it is my uninformed guess that trainers who don't like this technique have a back door and a back yard, so getting their dog outside in time is a lot easier. [Web search "bell training a dog" for more tips.]

## 4  Keys!

Oh, yes! (Well, that may not be exactly what you are saying to yourself.) The keys are on the kitchen counter, on the other side of one or more locked doors. And you are stuck outside with Spot. Now you have to wait for the next resident who happens along, or buzz the office or a resident with the hopes that someone is there to let you in.

It doesn't hurt to become good friends with a fellow resident or two who will be willing to let you in at any time of the night or day. But the best and most reliable strategy is to keep a key attached to the leash at all times. Pet stores usually have an assortment of little bags and boxes that attach to your dog's leash for your keys (another place to keep plastic poo bags, too). Or attach a key chain to the leash handle.

Never *ever* remove the key to your door(s) as long as you are using that leash. If you must "lose" your one allocated key in order to receive another one, well, "lose" your key. If your building uses key fobs or keycards instead of standard keys, figure out how to attach an extra one to your leash.

# 5 Carpets

This section is for those of you who have carpets and care about their condition (you are condo owners and apartment dwellers who want to get at least part of your initial deposit back). Not only will there be housebreaking accidents, but upset tummies make a yucky mess on the carpet, too.

Invest in a carpet shampooer! You can get small "spot shampooers" that are great for stairs and very, very small living spaces. But get a normal size one for larger spaces. Why? Cleaning the whole room will keep all parts of the carpet the same color. Otherwise you will end up with patches of different colors in places you probably won't want to put furniture.

This will be the best investment you make in the life of your dog. It will definitely reduce your stress level when accidents happen. You may be asking, "Where will I keep a carpet shampooer in my tiny living space?" I admit this can be an issue. They make handy coat trees. If you have a parking space in an attached parking structure, that's an option. I know of someone who keeps hers in the shower stall and moves it each day for shower time.

Nature's Miracle™ is a great spray spot cleaner for small jobs. You can use it when you don't have time to do the whole room or when you need to clean up in the hallway, lobby, or elevator. It does remove stains if you follow the directions, although you may need several applications. (Let me add this disclaimer: I have not received any incentive from the Nature's Miracle people. I suggest it because it works.)

## 6 Clean Up

What is the most important rule of urban dog etiquette? Clean up after your pooch. *Always*. No exceptions, *ever*. Mop up puddles on the (faux) marble floor in the lobby. Soak up puddles in the parking structure. For big messes, use that amazing carpet shampooer. Be sure to use it in the halls and elevators and stairwells, too. Never leave poo piles anywhere, especially in common spaces. Some people actually do leave poo piles and pee puddles around inside their buildings. That's just gross. This generally leads to the eviction of that dog owner, and sometimes to a general banishment of all dogs from the property. Don't leave poo piles outside, either—even at 2:00 in the morning in a blizzard. Even in the pouring rain. Even if it is just a tiny little bit. How do you like stepping in dog poo?

Get one of those little bags that attaches to your leash handle. It will hold plastic bags, treats, your clicker (research "clicker training"—for some dogs it can work miracles), business cards (yours and your dog trainer's), and your keys. The bags are great if you use a key card instead of a standard key for getting into your building. The bag should always be on the leash.

Even if you have a leash bag, keep plastic bags everywhere. Even if you are lucky enough to live in a city that has clean-up stations all around, keep plastic bags with you because sometime the stations are empty. Keep plastic bags by the door. Keep plastic bags in your car, in your purse, in your backpack, in your briefcase. Keep plastic bags in your pockets—all pockets at all times. Tie a plastic bag to the upper loop on the standard leash or to the handle of the retractable leash. This is not the situation to worry about being totally green. Poo piles are disgusting, dirty, yucky.

In some cities, you will experience *embarrassingly extreme peer pressure* if you try to walk away from your dog's pile. In other cities, people will just talk about you behind your back if you leave your dog's mess. And they *will* talk! You will be referred to as the DS guy or the DS girl when you are not around. (I'm sure you can figure out what DS stands for.)

There is a hard-to-miss sign in the yard of a duplex in my urban neighborhood: "Pick Up After Your Dog. It Is Your Responsibility, Not Ours." This sums up the thoughts of many an urban resident. "Not picking up after their dog" was the most common complaint I heard about dog owners when I was researching this book. "Leaving messes in hallways, stairwells, and parking areas" was the most common reason for banishing dogs that I heard from apartment owners and managers.

## 7 Resources

Read up on housebreaking in the dog training book of your choice or go online. There are lots of wonderful tips and tricks that apply to all puppies, no matter where they live. There are online resources for housebreaking an older dog, too. Remember that this is just a short phase in all the time you and your dog will spend together; when mistakes and accidents happen, don't stress over them.

## 8 Treats

Saving the best for last—treats. Lots and lots and lots of yummy, healthy little treats. Just like plastic bags, treats should always be on hand. Every single time your dog does its business in the right place at the right time, a wonderful reward is your immediate response. A treat, a "good dog," and a big hug are the best training tools you can use.

## ~ Eight Tips ~

## People

As the saying goes, there are all types of people in this world. If you are bringing a puppy to the city, your puppy will probably love most of the people it meets. If you are moving an older dog into the city, your dog may see more people in a few trips outside than it has seen in its entire life. You may learn, for the first time, how your older dog reacts to strangers.

### 1  Dog Dislikers

All right, let's get it out on the table at the start: Some people don't like dogs. They don't want to pet your dog. They don't want to talk to your dog. They definitely don't think your dog is cute or sweet. They don't *care* if your dog is friendly. They don't want to acknowledge the existence of your dog—unless it is misbehaving. They may mutter ugly things when walking by. We will skip over all judgments about such people. With war, poverty, disease, and disasters out there to worry about, we don't need to worry about people who don't like our dogs. There is only one tip that works with people who do not like dogs: Make sure your best friend behaves perfectly when those people are around. The rest of this book will give you some tips on how to do this.

## 2  Only My Dog

You, naturally, are not like this. But there are people who love their own dog but not your dog. Not anyone else's dog, just their own dog. What is *that* all about? There are two good things about people like this: They have a dog, and they love their dog. We must learn to co-exist happily with these people. And we must make double-sure that when we are near each other with our dogs, our best friend behaves better than theirs does. That last bit is just for our own satisfaction. They will neither notice nor care.

## 3  Dog Lovers—Without Dogs

When you are in a hurry, you may want to try to avoid people who love dogs but don't have dogs of their own. They will gush and goo-goo and ga-ga all over Fido. They will talk to your giant Rottweiler in baby talk. They will try to teach Fido terrible manners like jumping up and licking people's faces. They will tell you endless stories of every dog they ever had and how dogs love them and how they want to have a dog and why they don't have a dog. Smile. Adore them. Because they adore your best friend. Train Fido to love them. Give them treats to give to Fido. Pretend to listen for the umpteenth time as they tell you all about their sweet "may they rest in peace" former dogs. Why? First, it is good for Fido to know that you are not the only one who loves him. Second, some day that might be you. There may come a time when you want to hug a dog, but don't have one to hug.

What if Fido refuses to deal with these people, in spite of all the best encouragement and bribes you can provide? What if there never seems to be a time, day or night, when you can go out without one of these people there waiting for Fido? Dog lovers without their own dogs are everywhere; your only escape is to move to the middle of nowhere where there are no people. These dog lovers will never stop trying to be your dog's best friend. That is a wonderful thing, and we are lucky to have them around.

## 4  Pickled People

Friday and Saturday nights, and most any lovely evening, bring on the pub crawl. Of course Sadie the Saluki will need to go out for a walk at some point in the evening. After a few too many drinks, many people, including even the firmest dog haters, seem to love dogs. However, some dogs that normally love people do not feel the same affinity for people who have had too much to drink. Try to get to the other side of the street to avoid a group of over-imbibers if you can. If you must go through a crowd of tipsy people, just repeat loudly and clearly, over and over, that your dog is not at all friendly and that it needs to potty right now. That will generally clear a path for you. A blurry-brained few won't get it, but their buddies will generally pull them out of the way. This is not the time for you to be timid. This is not the time to amble or mumble. Put on your game face, crank up your voice volume, and stride ahead at a good clip with Sadie trotting along right beside you.

## 5  People In Uniforms

Some dogs, for whatever little doggie-brain reasons, go berserk when they see someone in a uniform. The best way to manage this is to divert their behavior to something positive.

If Snoozer only learns a few tricks in his entire life, one of them must be this three-part trick. It's performed on silent cues whenever a uniformed person is nearby:

- *Bow!* with great flourish
- Wag his tail enthusiastically while in the bow
- Move immediately from *Bow!* to *Sit!*, then to *Sit And Stay!* until you give him the silent command to get up.

If you don't think you can manage this, a simple *Sit And Stay!* will work.

In a lot of cities, many police officers, firefighters, and mail carriers carry treats with them, so Snoozer's display of respect might be rewarded. Snoozer will definitely be placed notches higher than those dogs that bark and snap.

> If your dog is off leash, or if you have just walked away from not having picked up after your dog, no amount of cute will salvage your reputations with police officers. You may find yourself holding a ticket and owing a hefty fine.

## 6 Perfect People

Perfect people love all dogs, including yours. They have a well-trained dog of their own. As time goes by, you will learn to love and appreciate these people beyond all others in your neighborhood. Some of these perfect people might not be people-people, so striking up a conversation with them might not be in the cards. Others are, and you and your dog will make some wonderful lifelong friends.

## 7  Children

Dogs and children can be a volatile mix. Not all dogs love children. Even if your dog is one of those "my dog is friendly" dogs and is accustomed to having children around all the time, your dog might not love other people's children. Not all children love dogs. Not all parents want their children to have close encounters with your dog or anyone else's dog. On the other hand, some parents *want* their children to have close encounters with any and all dogs, including yours. They might force their children on your dog even when you are screeching at them that your dog is evil and will bite their child's arm off. There *is* potential for something bad to happen. You must be the responsible adult in the group when it comes to your dog and someone else's children. (After repeated encounters with clueless parents, you will begin to appreciate parents who train their children to ask permission from you before trying to pet your dog.)

It is highly possible that nothing awful will happen during close encounters between your dog and someone else's child. It is highly possible that your dog and someone else's child will hit it off and have a wonderful time together. On the other hand, things might not go that well. Keep in mind that if the parent even imagines that your dog bit the child, it will be your fault entirely. That will be true even if the child bit a hole in your dog's ear and the dog only whimpered a tiny bit. If the parent decides that your dog did something to the child, true or not true, you could end up with a major problem. This is discussed in more detail in the Tags, Licenses, and Health & Legal Whatnot chapter.

## 8  Treats

Treats are a wonderful way to encourage your dog to deal with all sorts of people. When Fido is an angel around people who don't like him, give him a treat. When he puts up with the goo-gooers and ga-gaggers, give him a treat. When Snoozer doesn't bark at the mail carrier, he gets a treat. When you manage to get Sadie through a tipsy crowd, give her a treat for trotting along and not becoming distracted.

## ~ Seven Tips ~
## Dogs, Cats, And Other Urban Critters

Living in a city includes living with dogs, cats, potbelly piglets, monkeys, horses, and other critters people have and love. Helping your dog live in peace with them is part of the excitement of city life with a dog. Encounters with them will be the source of many a story you will tell friends and family for years to come.

### 1  Monster Dog

Just as there are people who don't like dogs, there are dogs that don't like other dogs. There are dogs that don't like people. There are people who have dogs and love them, but don't train them well. Some badly trained dogs are simply annoying. But some badly trained dogs are a menace. Avoid these dogs.

You will learn to notice Monster Dog from blocks away. The first time you saw it, it was the dog pulling its owner along at breakneck speed or tugging with all its might on the leash. As soon as it saw your dog, it started snarling and barking. Or worse, it was the dog that was minding its manners nicely until you and your dog walked by. Then you heard the snarling, saw the barred teeth, and worse—saw the snapping. Meet Surprise Monster Dog.

Cross the street when you see Monster Dog coming. Turn around and dash to a different street. Or go through the nearest open door—even if you risk being yelled at by whoever is on the other side. Do whatever it takes to avoid being on the same sidewalk at the same time.

If Monster Dog is your beloved Vlad, make sure he is leashed and glued to your side when you must take him out. Firmly and loudly tell other dog owners that Vlad is not friendly *before* they let their dog dash toward him. You must say this very firmly and very loudly because some dog owners are totally clueless. They will say something completely irrelevant such as, "Oh, my dog is friendly." Be sure that people who try to pet him are also fully informed. If you see children ahead, you must cross the street or turn around.

*Do* take it personally when other dog owners cross the street or turn and run or disappear into buildings when they see you coming. Deal with it if someone tells you to your face that you need to do something about your dog. They are not being rude; they are doing you a favor.

It is not someone else's problem. The worst thing you can do is to ignore the problem, thinking it will go away. Just as bad is to be in denial and think it is not a problem. At some point Vlad might injure someone, someone's child, or someone's pet. You will be in court. Vlad will be on death row.

The best thing you can do is to contact a dog trainer who specializes in working with this type of dog. Your vet or your local Humane Society will be able to recommend someone.

## 2  Overly Friendly Dogs

Some dogs are exuberant and sweet and leap forward to greet all dogs they see. They love everyone and are impossible not to love in return (if you love other people's dogs).

But they are a problem for people who don't like dogs. They are a problem for people who have a nonvisible handicap such as arthritis or a bone or muscle disease or an injury. They are a huge problem for people who are afraid of dogs. And they risk their safety around dogs that have issues (like Monster Dog). One more thing to think about: Any dog can become a monster dog if it thinks its owner is being threatened or is in danger. If your dog leaps forward toward a person-pet pair, the other person's dog might go into protective mode instead of play mode.

If this wonderful exuberant bouncing bundle of fur is yours, keep trying. No matter how many dog training classes you and Bouncer are kicked out of, keep trying. There are great new collar technologies. There are methods of training that will work for you and your dog. There is a trainer out there who can help.

Meanwhile, work out who is in charge. That would be you. Bouncer must know, understand, and truly believe that fact. The "walk the other way" trick helps your dog learn that you are the one in charge. When Bouncer starts to pull you forward to greet the dog coming toward you, simply turn around and walk in the opposite direction. Don't worry about whether or not the person–pet pair coming toward you will have their feelings hurt because you suddenly went off in a different direction. If Bouncer is a pouncer and waits until another dog is right next to you before leaping up in greeting, then make this a habit:

- Stop walking when you see a person–pet pair coming toward you.
- Have Bouncer sit and stay right up against your leg until the temptation has walked past.
- Let the other person–pet pair know, *before* they get to you, that they must keep walking; they must not stop to chat because you are trying to train Bouncer.

## 3  Guide Dogs And Service Dogs

This should not need to be said, but it is surprising how many people do not control their dogs around guide dogs and service dogs.

So here it is: No matter how exuberantly your dog loves other dogs and wants to play, no matter how gentle and loving it is, you must keep it totally under control when a guide dog or a service dog is present. Again: You may have the friendliest, most wonderful dog in the world, but it must be totally under control around a guide dog or a service dog.

Sorry to have to say it twice, but people who use guide or service dogs have stories to tell about people (and their dogs) who do not respect their needs. That is a sad state of affairs.

If a service dog owner invites your dog to play, then, and only then, is it OK. But just because one or two service dog owners invite your dog to play with theirs doesn't mean it is common for all service dog owners. Wait for an invitation and don't feel hurt if you don't get one.

## 4  Horses

People moving into a city from anywhere else are saying, "Horses????" Yes, lots of cities have lots of horses. Mounted police and horse-drawn carriages will be everyday sights for you and your dog in many urban areas.

City horses are well trained to ignore barking dogs. Even so, do whatever you can to teach your dog not to bark at them. Barking dogs are annoying to everyone around. (Read more about that in the chapter on Barking.)

If your dog is on a leash, it won't be able to dash over and nip at the horses' ankles. If it is not on a leash, and if it does dash toward the horse, a whole lot of unhappiness will ensue for you, your pet, the horse, and the rider or the carriage driver. A lot of unhappiness.

It's one more excellent reason to keep your beloved pet on a leash.

## 5  Chipmunks, Squirrels, Geese

Chipmunks and squirrels and geese are fascinating and there is nothing some dogs would rather do than chase them. Remember, dogs are predators. But it's not allowed. Hunter should not be allowed to dash gleefully though the park chasing squirrels and chipmunks and geese. Dogs dashing around the park put too many people and other pets at risk. A dog after a squirrel will not pay attention around children or elderly people. A dog after a squirrel could follow the squirrel into the street. The dashing dog is much more likely to be hit by a car than the dashing squirrel.

Nor is everyone is amused by Hunter standing at the base of a tree barking like crazy at a squirrel. Ponder this: Would you want the surgeon who is trying to sleep in the unit near the tree to operate on you or someone you know in an emergency situation later on that day?

As for geese? They are big and some are downright mean. Depending on the size of your dog, the goose or gander could be the winner in a confrontation. (The same goes for swans, which are common in a few cities.) In some cities, dogs are used to control geese on beaches, on golf courses, and in parks. Some people are very much against this. But if you are comfortable with this, and think it is something you would like your dog to do, then look into volunteering your dog. Your dog could have a job doing what he loves to do in an authorized and controlled manner.

## 6 Other Non-Dogs

In some cities, you and your dog are likely to encounter cats and pot-belly piglets and monkeys and all manner of species out for a stroll, hanging around the park, or attending pet-friendly events. Your dog's true nature will suddenly go into full gear, so don't let this first encounter surprise you. Be realistic here. Your dog is a dog. Dogs are predators and they will behave true to their nature, no matter how much you might want to believe otherwise.

Additionally, you don't have a clue how well trained the other critter is. Some broad generalizations apply:

- Monkeys tend to be aggressive, so it is probably a bad idea to let the monkey and the dog get close.
- Pot-belly pigs are not aggressive, but your dog may be a danger to the pig.
- Cats and dogs sometimes get along, but sometimes don't.

Some species can transmit nasty diseases to other species; however cute a close encounter may be for two well-behaved critters, they could actually make each other sick.

Often when there is an issue, the nearest dog is blamed, even when it is not the dog's fault. Not fair, but often true. Having considered all this, if you still think you want your dog to have a close encounter with a critter and the critter's owner is agreeable, do so with full knowledge of the potential risk.

Some dogs will be absolutely fascinated. Let the critter's owner take the lead and notify you whether a close encounter is wise and the best way to go about it. You must be totally relaxed, because Nosey will definitely pick up any vibes you send down the leash. You must be alert, cautious, in total control, and ready to yank Nosey away in a nanosecond. If you are nervous, don't even try to introduce them. If things go well, you will have met a new walking companion and Nosey might have a new friend.

Some dogs should never be allowed to attempt a close encounter of any kind with any critter. If this is your dog, deal with the critter in exactly the same way you would deal with Monster Dog—cross the street or dive into the nearest doorway or walk the other way. Because you are naturally paying close attention to the situation, you will know when your dog has moved into some type of hyper mode and will not be at all friendly with the critter in question. The critter owner has been around the block more than once, is not clueless, and will be grateful if you pull your pet out of a situation with the potential for causing harm or being harmed.

Don't feel guilty. By avoiding disaster you have done the right thing.

## 7  Treats

Of course, you have a pocketful of treats to be handed out liberally while your dog is walking nicely. Give him a treat when he doesn't yank you in the direction of a chipmunk, squirrel, or goose. Give hugs, praise, and treats when the horses clop by and your dog doesn't bark. There are so many wonderful opportunities for treats when out for a walk in the city—no wonder dogs love going for walks.

## ~ Six Tips ~
## Absolutely Critical Commands And Related Topics

The importance of training class for your dog is stressed throughout the book. It is so much easier to learn to work with your dog when you have real-life examples and when an expert can work directly with you and your dog. It's interesting to know that most professional dog trainers and dog breeders attend training class when they get a new puppy. These are professional trainers! Going to dog training class does not mean that you don't know how to train your dog. It means that you have a new puppy with a personality that is different from all other dogs you have had. It means that you want to get up to speed on the latest training techniques. It means you want to devote an hour each week to having fun with your dog. It means taking your dog to a weekly event that it will enjoy more than anything in its little life. It means meeting a lot of great dog owners.

There are puppy schools in most cities. I recommend the local Humane Society, if they offer classes and if they are convenient for you. They have very knowledgeable trainers, and are sometimes more reasonably priced than private classes. Your class fees go right back into the organization, allowing it to offer more classes. There are many excellent private classes and one-on-one dog trainers out there also. Ask around and get recommendations from people you know and people whose opinion about dogs you respect. That said, let's move along.

Your city dog must know *Leave it!* and *Drop it!* and *Heel!* for its own safety, your safety, and the safety of other people and pets. Because *Come!*, *Down!*, *Sit!*, and *Stay!* are covered thoroughly in puppy classes and in training books, they won't be covered in detail here. But make sure your dog knows these commands, too.

If your city is like most, the sidewalks have stuff your dog will really, really, really want to taste—partially eaten hot dogs, cigarette butts, melting ice cream, pieces of gum, fluffs of cotton candy, popcorn, and all sorts of things you'd rather not name. None of these is something you want your dog putting in its mouth. So *Leave it!* and *Drop it!* are essential. You also need to be aware of plants and grasses that your dog loves to munch on. They can be just as bad for your dog as the yucky food and other stuff on the sidewalks and streets—or worse.

*Heel!* is thoroughly covered in training classes, but it is included in this survival guide because keeping your dog under control all times is so important in a city, where you should always expect the unexpected.

Teaching these critical commands takes a lot of practice. It is best done initially in a place with minimal distractions—at home, not in the park. Practice at least once a day, every day. Practice two or three times a day when you can. It is fairly easy to fit a couple of sessions in between work and bedtime. Some of the drills are short enough that you can fit a quick session in before work. Perform each drill four to ten times in one training session, depending on the complexity of the drill and your dog's attention span (about five to ten minutes).

In addition to practice, teaching these commands also requires a lot of patience. As much as you really might want to at times, don't yell at your dog or throw a temper tantrum. Anyone who has trained a dog will tell you that it can be tempting. One more thing: Your dog does not know this is "training". You can make it fun for your dog by using treats and lots of hugs. Think of it as teaching your dog nifty tricks that result in a dog that is fun to take out and that gets lots of attention for being so good. If you attend training class, ask the teacher whether *Drop it!* and *Leave it!* drills will be included. If these commands will not be covered in detail in class, the teacher might be willing to work on them with you and your dog before or after class.

To make sure the training sticks, and for your own sanity, don't try to teach your dog all of these commands at once. If you are taking a class, follow the pace of the class. If you have decided to do the training on your own with a book, work on one command at a time. When your dog has mastered one command, move on to the next. There are lots of dog training "methods". This chapter presents an overview of the generic basics for these commands. Your teacher or the book you are using may have a different approach.

## 1  Leave It!

*Leave it!* is used every time you see something you know your dog will love, but something it should not put in its mouth. Say it in the most commanding voice you are capable of producing.

> Do not give your dog treats during *Leave it!* training. You want your dog to understand that it must not eat this food. Dogs are good at assigning meanings to words on their own, so if you let your dog have the training treats, she may learn that *Leave it!* means "wait" or "later" or some other thing her little doggie brain might come up with. Hugs and rubs and lots of verbal reinforcement will work just fine.

1. The first step in this training sequence is to put a lovely treat in the palm of your hand and show it to Doodles. When she tries to grab it, say, *"Leave it!"* and close your hand. Do this three or four times during one training session. That's it. You have finished for this session. Have a training session at least once a day. You may be able to squeeze in a session in before work without having to get up any earlier. When

Doodles doesn't even think about grabbing the treat out of your hand, she is ready for the next steps.

2. Have Doodles, on her leash, sit right next to you. You will have a great treat in one hand and her leash firmly in your other hand.

3. Show Doodles the treat and say, *"Doodles, leave it!"* She knows what to do (what not to do). Now drop the treat right in front of her. When she goes for it, use the leash to stop her and say, *"Leave it!"*

4. While she sits there a few seconds, wanting the treat but not trying to grab it (she can't while you hang on to the leash), tell her how wonderful she is and what a good dog she is and give her a hug.

5. Turn her around, pick up the treat, and go through the drill again. Do this two or three times for one training session. Have at least one training session each day.

6. When Doodles behaves perfectly while she is sitting next to you, you can begin to make the training sessions a little harder by moving a few steps away from her (leash still firmly in your hand).

7. When Doodles can be a perfect pooch, make the training harder by stepping even farther away from her.

If, at any point, Doodles digresses, back up the training and work on the easy steps for a few more sessions.

8. When you can move as far away from her as the leash will allow, it is time to step it up another notch. Drop your end of the leash on the floor before you take a few steps away. Practice this for several sessions, stepping farther and farther away from Doodles and the leash each time.

9. Then give her more of a challenge: do this with Doodles entirely off of her leash. If she digresses when off the leash, go back to the drill with leash on for a few more sessions.

10. When Doodles is a perfect pooch off the leash, start using much stronger temptations—her favorite toy, a peanut butter sandwich, cheese, chicken, whatever she will really, really want. You may need to back up a few steps with this greater temptation.

11. Now you are ready for Top Dog level training. Instead of having Doodles sitting nicely, practice walking around with Doodles on the leash and treats scattered around on the floor. As you approach a treat, say, *"Leave it!"* Soon Doodles will be able to do this, too.

You will know Doodles is perfectly trained in *Leave it!* when you can create a pathway of incredible treats and toys and walk her down "Temptation Trail" and she does not attempt to pick up a single thing.

At this point, you are probably thinking that it will take at least a year to accomplish all these steps. Not to worry. If you work on this every day, it won't take very long. You will be able to accomplish more than one step in a day. If you can practice several times a day, Doodles will have this trick down in no time.

When you and Doodles are out in the real world and she walks by a temptation on the sidewalk, be sure you praise her, give her a treat, hug her, and do everything you can to make sure she knows she is a wonderful, wonderful dog. [Web search "leave it command" for more tips.]

## 2  Drop It!

Use *Drop it!* every time you weren't able to say *Leave it!* before your dog got something nasty in its mouth. This command must be used *before* your dog swallows whatever it has picked up.

Say *Drop it!* in the same commanding voice you use for *Leave it!* The key to success with *Drop it!* is your excellent timing. It may not be so good in the beginning, but you will get the hang of it. You should have at least one short training session each day; several would be better.

1. Step one in teaching *Drop it!* is to determine Droopy's favorite treat in the whole wide world. Liver treat? Peanut butter flavor dog bone? Salmon flavor? Whatever it is, use it for training.

2. Step two is to find a toy Droopy will hold in his mouth.

Essentially you will be teaching Droopy that when he has something in his mouth and you say, *"Drop it!"*, you will exchange whatever he had in his mouth for something even better. You are going to give him a higher-value item in exchange for a lower-value item. Even if Droopy is the dimmest bulb in the chandelier, he will catch on to this trick with lightening speed.

3. Get Droopy's toy and start to play with him. When he has the toy firmly in his mouth, pass that wonderful treat in front of his nose. Unless you've picked the wrong treat, Droopy will take the treat and the toy will fall out of his mouth. Do this two or three times to get the drill down.

4. Now you will give Droopy his toy. Pass the treat in front of his nose. As he opens his mouth, you say *"Drop it!"* in a seriously commanding voice. He drops the toy. He gets the treat. Do this six to ten times, depending on his attention span, and then play with him.

5. After several days of practicing step 4, give Droopy a toy and say *"Drop it!"* without passing the treat in front of his nose. If he does not drop the toy, keep practicing step 4. If he does drop the toy, tell him how wonderful he is and give him his wonderful treat. Keep practicing.

6. When you think he has step 5 down, make it a bit harder. Give Droopy a toy, say *"Drop it!"*, and make him wait for the treat. Or maybe he doesn't even get

a treat this time. Keep doing the drill, but reward him randomly or walk away and come back with the reward. You are teaching him to drop whatever is in his mouth whether he gets paid for it or not.

7. This step is even harder. Droopy will be asked to drop something he loves, but his reward will be something even better. Put something wonderful on the floor. When he picks it up, command him sternly to *Drop it! You* must be perfect with your timing. You don't want him to confuse *Drop it!* with *Leave it!*. But you must get the *Drop it!* command out before Droopy eats the entire training treat and there is nothing left to drop. Work on this until Droopy will drop something he loves without a treat reward (hugs and praise are always appropriate). You may need to back up to step 4, step 5, or step 6 for a while. But keep working.

You know Droopy is perfectly trained in *Drop it!* when you can repeatedly give him the most wonderful piece of food in his world and he spits it out the instant you say "*Drop it!*" This means he will spit out a peanut butter sandwich. He will spit out a piece of chicken. He will spit out anything that he has in his mouth.

Even when Droopy drops anything at anytime he is told to do so, it is a good idea to keep reinforcing this command. You can reinforce *Drop it!* when you play fetch with your dog. When he brings back the stick or ball or whatever, say *"Drop it!"* instead of pulling it out of his mouth. Reinforce *Drop it!* while your dog is playing around with his toys.

When you are out in the real city world and Droopy drops on command, praise him, hug him, and give him a treat. Be sure that you always reward him for obeying the *Drop it!* command. [Web search "drop it command" for more tips.]

## 3  Heel!

Use *Heel!* to command your dog to trot right next to your leg, as though he were stuck to you with Velcro. It is exactly what it says—your dog's little front paws are at about the same place as your heels when you are both standing still. It is critical for your dog to heel when you walk down a crowded sidewalk. He must heel when you are walking past sidewalk cafe tables and park benches populated with people trying to eat. He must heel in every situation that requires him to be under your total control while walking.

In the beginning, practice *Heel!* where there are few distractions: your apartment, along the apartment hallways, and the parking structure (if you are lucky enough to have one of those).

While you are training *Heel!*, don't stress if your dog is better at this at home than when out in the real world. Real-world distractions can make it hard for her to concentrate when she is learning this trick. Naturally she will be out and about before she has learned *Heel!* completely. When you start training indoors, don't worry about what happens when you are outside. As she gets better at this command indoors, you can begin practicing outside in low-stress, minimal-chaos situations. Soon she will be able to heel nicely wherever she is. She will be ready to go out and about with you anywhere she is allowed, provided she wants to be there (more about this in the Events section).

Some training materials and classes teach you to walk your dog on your left side. Some let you pick which side you want to walk your dog on, but ask that you be consistent. A city dog must be able to walk well on both sides of you. When negotiating city sidewalks and city crowds and trying to get across city streets, sometimes one side is more appropriate for your dog than the other.

Stick to one side while doing the initial training. After your dog has mastered the basic *Heel!* command, you can introduce the concept of walking on either side of you. If you want to teach your dog commands for this, use the basic *Heel!* for one side. Introduce *Heel right!* or *Heel left!* for walking on the other side. This training will go a little faster because your dog already knows the basic concept. Just be consistent with whatever command you select for heeling on each side.

Ultimately the cue for Harvey to move to your other side will probably be nonverbal signals or how you are holding the leash, but verbal commands are handy. Bottom line, Harvey can learn how to heel perfectly on both sides of you.

What is the secret to teaching the *Heel!* command? Patience! (Remember, start out in a place that has the fewest opportunities for your dog to become confused and for you to become frustrated.)

What are the steps?

1. Put a ton of treats in your pocket.

2. Put the leash on Harvey. Start with a normal leash and collar. When you step out into the real world, you will know right away whether you are going to need a more controlling collar. Initially, start out with a normal leash and collar combination.

3. With Harvey on his leash, place him at your side. You should both be facing in the same direction. This sounds like a no-brainer, but isn't always as simple as it sounds. At first, Harvey will probably want to stand facing you or sideways. When you and Harvey are facing the same direction, hold the leash in both hands. The hand farthest from Harvey is holding the top loop end and tiny treats. The hand closest to Harvey is holding the leash near Harvey's collar.

4. Once in position, establish eye contact with Harvey (say his name to get him to look up at you). Take a couple of steps forward, and stop. If Harvey moves forward with you, staying right by your side, praise him without restraint and give him a treat. If he just stands there, don't be impatient with him. Just back up and try again.

5. Try this again—just a few steps forward. And again. And again, taking a few more steps each time.

6. If Harvey lags behind or bounds ahead or trundles off in an entirely different direction, don't say a word. Just go back to the starting place and the starting position, and try again. Your patience is the key here. If you try several times and he just doesn't get it, stop and try again another time. You don't want to yell at Harvey or make him think he is being

a bad dog. He is just learning, and it sometimes tries the patience of people teaching this command.

7. When Harvey is able to trot along beside you for about ten steps every time, begin to attach the verbal cue *Heel!* Do the same drill, but a second before you take the first step, say, *"Harvey, heel!"*

8. When Harvey has learned to *"Heel!"* without any mistakes, it is time to increase the challenge. Try some variations on the theme—one at a time, so he learns each one. Try walking slowly, walking quickly, running, turning right, turning left, walking around stuff. Don't forget to give him a treat every few minutes to reward him for being so good.

> Learning to walk around stuff is an important part of training *Heel!* for city living. When you are out walking Harvey in the real world, he has to stay next to you as you walk around stuff. You will not want him wandering around to the other side of a lamp post or a parking meter or a person while you are holding one end of the leash and he is attached to the other end. Very klutzy.

Now it is time to work on the *Heel!* command outside on the city sidewalks and in the park. Lots of treats and praise are in order when Harvey is behaving correctly. If Harvey forgets and tries to charge ahead, you should suddenly turn around and walk in the opposite direction. Or stop and walk backward a few steps. Or just stop. Reel him back in, get him pointed in the right direction, and say, "*Harvey, Heel!*" Harvey will learn that these are cues for him to pay attention and stick with you. Keep treats in the pocket that is on the side Harvey generally walks on. Give him lots of little treats for being good. Harvey will learn that whenever he is being good and your hand goes in the pocket, treats appear. If Harvey is a normal dog, his nose won't stray too far from the pocketful of treats.

Sometimes in a city it is necessary to get your dog's attention and immediately change pace. By using variations on the *Heel!* command, you can communicate these situations. For example, you can use *Heel quick!* to let Harvey know that suddenly the two of you can't lollygag along anymore. You can use *Heel slow!* to get his attention if you need to slow down suddenly. If Harvey is good at *Heel!*, he will constantly adapt to your walking speed anyway. But there are situations when you want to make absolutely sure he is with you in a change of pace. These variations can be introduced one at a time after Harvey is really good at the basic *Heel!* command. It is amazing how fluent dogs can become in people talk. If only we could become that good at dog talk. [Web search "heel command" for more tips.]

> If you use *Hurry up!* as a housebreaking cue word, don't use it when you want him to move along more quickly. Harvey will wonder what you really want him to do (especially if he just finished doing his business and you told him what a good boy he was).

Absolutely Critical Commands And Related Topics

## 4  *Come!* And *Down and stay!* On Command

Because they are more complex than the three commands already discussed, I will not go into detail about these two commands in this small survival guide. They are best taught in training class. They are also covered extensively in dog training books and on the Internet. If you decide not to take a training class with your dog, you can find the information there. But they are critical commands that you and your dog *must* know.

Your city pup should be taught to respond immediately to these commands off leash in the midst of distractions. In spite of all your diligence and best intentions, there could come a time when Dasher gets loose and starts racing around being a dog.

You truly do not want Dasher running into the street if he gets loose. Use the *Come!* command when the two of you are on the same side of the street and he is fairly close to you. He should be taught to race right back to you without a thought. Use *Down and stay!* when Dasher manages to cross the street without being hit. You definitely don't want to push your luck and have him cross the street back to you on his own. Use *Down and stay!* when Dasher is farther away than a few steps, and when he has that look in his eyes that he is moving into Wild Child mode. Use it when he must freeze in place until you get to him.

> If you use *Down!* as the command for him to "lie down," use a different command when he jumps up on someone. You can use *Drop!* to tell him to lie down. You can use *Off!* to tell him to take his paws off of someone. Pick words that are easy for you to remember and use them consistently. Dogs will learn whatever words we teach them. Fortunately, they won't repeat some of them in polite company.

Work on these commands with Dasher at home until he is perfect. Work with him out and about, on his leash, until he is perfect. The next step is to practice these commands in the park with Dasher on a long lead. Long leads are very, very long leashes that are often made of very flimsy fabric. Some people prefer clothesline rope because it's stronger. Check with your dog trainer about the best techniques for using a long lead with your dog, because some dogs can turn into Wild Child when given this much slack.

There is a huge leap to the next stage of training—the dog park or dog run. Some dogs are absolutely perfect at *Come!* or *Down and stay!* until they are out with their buddies. You may wonder if all the excellent training you did for months was some sort of a dream you had. Wonderful treats are helpful, but some dogs don't give a flip about treats when they can play with their friends.

If you need one good reason to take your dog to training class, teaching the *Come!* and *Down and stay!* commands is that reason. The other dogs in the class provide the distractions you need to really get this training right. And the teacher and other dog owners are there to catch your dog, if necessary, as he zooms around. If you take Dasher to doggie day care, ask them to reinforce these commands with him periodically.

## 5  Collars And Leashes

> Neither a collar, nor a leash, nor a combination of both, will train your dog. They are simply tools to help you keep your dog doing what you have already trained it to do.

There are new collar technologies that are less aggressive than choke chains and prong collars. When used properly, they are equally or even more effective. Harness collars (with the leash attachment in the front on your dog's chest) and head collars (with a loop that fits around the nose) are both amazing for keeping your dog under control.

Double-loop leashes are good for when you need a little more control. One loop forms the traditional hand hold at the top end of the leash. The lower loop provides a secure hand hold just above the collar. You can keep your dog right next to you, and you won't worry about the lower part of the leash slipping in your hand. If you have an exuberant dog and are using a head collar, you might want to use a double-loop leash, too. They don't work as well with harness collars because the lower loop might be out of your reach and because it is easy for your dog to trip over it.

Retractable leashes are not effective in situations where it is important that you keep your dog in good control. In fact, there are not many city situations where a retractable leash is an appropriate option. You may not want to hear that, but it is just too hard to get your dog to your side quickly in an emergency situation if you are using a retractable leash.

When you get Harvey outside in the real world, he will be expected to *Heel!* under lots of different conditions. This is when you will find out whether you need a harness or a head collar or a double-loop leash. Harvey may be perfect at home but an entirely different dog outside. Each of these wonderful inventions helps keep Harvey right by your side with all four paws on the ground. Talk with your vet or dog trainer about which collar would be best, and try out various types. As for the double-loop leash, it is truly a wonderful invention. [Web search "dog harness", "head collar", "double loop leash".]

> If you decide to try a head collar, don't expect your dog to love it. It probably won't. But don't give up too soon. Some dogs never adjust so a harness collar is a better option. Other dogs do learn to wear head collars without struggle and drama. Head collars make walks with energetic dogs so much easier.

## 6  Treats And Play

Be sure to have a play session after every training session (except maybe the really quick ones before work). Your pet will look forward to learning. Treats are great, and dogs do love treats. But nothing beats petting him and hugging him and letting him chase toys that you toss.

When your wonderful dog knows all of these commands completely, he deserves lots of treats when you go on a walk and he shows you and everyone around how good he is. He also needs lots of ongoing verbal reinforcement: *"Good girl to heel!" "Good boy to leave it!"*

## ~ Five Tips ~
## Sidewalk Cafes, Stores, Flowers, And Vehicles

Life in the city provides lots of challenging experiences for you and your dog. Sometimes walking along the sidewalk feels like negotiating a maze. Crossing a street can make you think you are in the middle of an action adventure film. Just sitting and watching the world go by is rarely boring.

### 1 Sidewalk Cafes

Knowing the *Leave it!* command and being able to walk on either side of you are essential skills your dog must have when negotiating the ubiquitous sidewalk cafe. Dino the Dinosaur Dog should know that he must stay away from the tables, even when there is hardly enough space to get by them. He definitely should not look as though he's thinking about sampling a salad or sticking his nose into a plate of nachos. Any dog with a table-high head can make outdoor cafe diners nervous. For that matter, so can a purse pet who is peeking out of a table-high purse. It is up to you to handle your dog in a way that reassures people that their food will be safe.

If you have to start saying *Leave it!* and continue saying it loudly and nonstop until you pass all the tempting tables, then that is what you must do. People won't think you're an insane babbling idiot, they will be grateful.

The great thing about teaching your dog to mind its manners in sidewalk cafes is that many of them allow well-behaved dogs to stay nicely under the table or under a chair or in a purse while the owners enjoy the fare. I've heard of a Great Dane who lives in Manhattan and often sits on a chair at a sidewalk cafe table with his owner for breakfast. I can't promise that many cafe owners will be that understanding about our best friends, but rumor has it that there is at least one.

## 2  Stores And Other Small Businesses

It is amazing how many dog-friendly establishments there are in cities. Hardware stores and pet stores seem to be especially open to canine customers. Some bookstores and office supply stores are pet friendly. Be sure to ask before bringing Fluffy inside. The friendliest, most well-behaved dog in the world may not be welcome inside because other dog owners took advantage of the situation. Or management may be sensitive to employees or customers who have dander allergies. Please don't take it personally if you are not allowed to bring your dog inside.

If Fluffy is welcome, *Leave it!* is the most wonderful phrase in any language known to dog and man. Naturally Fluffy should not pull things off of shelves or out of bins. And naturally Fluffy should not go on an off-leash romp up and down the aisles. In most cases, if Fluffy has been an angel, she will be given a wonderful treat and invited to return when you both leave.

Don't even think about taking Fluffy into a food store or deli—even if she is a purse-pet. Once again, don't take it personally. Having a dog inside is a quick way for your favorite market or deli to get in trouble with the health department. Most outdoor markets allow dogs, though. Sidewalk cafe manners are in order for outdoor markets.

## 3  Flowers And Plants

Flower boxes and flower pots and flower beds are not for dogs. Dogs should not munch on the contents; they should not use them as littler boxes. It is so sad to see a dog tromping around in someone's flowers, doing its thing, and then flipping little plants into the air with its back feet doing the post-poo back leg shuffle.

Many people love their plants just as much as you love your dog. They make a significant financial investment in them. They talk to their plants and flowers. They feed and water their plants and flowers, just like you feed and water your dog. They would take them for walks if they could. How would you like it if a green and purple thing took a bite out of your Sweetie Pie or relieved itself all over her or flipped her into the air?

And don't forget: The contents of the flower boxes or pots or beds could make Sweetie Pie violently ill if she decides to take a bite. Some plants are poisonous; some people use herbicides and pesticides on their plants.

## 4  Vehicles

I'm sure when I start naming the kinds of vehicles in a city, I will leave some out: skates and skateboards, inline skates, bicycles, motorcycles, Segways, cars, busses, trucks, trolleys, horse-drawn carts and carriages. The first few probably don't technically qualify as "vehicles," but they are things with wheels. When they zip by, dogs can become excited or frightened or get in trouble.

Skateboards make a lot of noise and spook some dogs. If there are a lot of them in your area, your dog will eventually get used to them. Until then, be prepared for either passive or aggressive behavior from your dog. Some puppies are totally terrified of skateboards.

People on roller skates or inline skates seem to confuse some dogs. In other dogs, they stir a chasing instinct. If you have a chaser and are in an area with a lot of skaters, keep your pooch glued to your side. Most skaters are oblivious to the impact they have on dogs, so it will be up to you to pay attention for them. Some skaters have a dog with them, racing ahead or trotting way behind. Accident potential! If you skate with your dog, *Heel!* still applies and it helps prevent accidents.

Some cities have well-informed cyclists, making everything so much safer for everyone. If you hear "on your right" or "on your left," that means the cyclist is coming from behind you on that side. You must get yourself and your dog out of the way. Some cyclists ding a little bell that they come up behind you. Even though you need to turn around to see where they are, at least they give a warning. Some bicyclists are oblivious to the fact that a spooked dog can cause a major accident and they don't warn you. Others think you have eyes in the back of your head, so they yell at you for not getting out of their way. If you are in an area where you share the sidewalk or path with bicyclists, it is up to you to be the responsible person and keep your dog stuck to your side.

Some cyclists zip along streets and sidewalks with their dog on a leash attached to the bike. I know how much fun it is to cycle with your dog, but if you are this person, have a good think about the potential for trouble that exists when a dog trots along next to a bike on a street or sidewalk in a city. It's unsafe for so many reasons, and it violates most leash laws. Plus, it might not be all that good for your dog's hips and paws. Check with your vet about this. If your vet thinks it is OK for your dog to run alongside while you cycle for a specific distance, there are places other than city streets and sidewalks where you can do so more safely. Not so convenient, I admit, but safer.

Busses, trolleys, and trucks make a lot of noise for sensitive doggie ears, and puppies are often afraid at first. In time, most dogs sort them out just fine. Some dogs seem fascinated by people getting off busses and by people disappearing into them. Some dogs just don't like trolleys and won't ever like trolleys and that is that. The clatter, the bells—something sets them off. If this is your dog, refer to the Barking section and work with your dog to keep it from barking too much at the trolleys.

Anything being pulled by a horse can set some dogs off into a barking and jumping frenzy. If this is your dog and it's at all possible, find a spot where you can stand or sit with your dog and work to calm it down. The section on Barking offers some tips. Keep in mind that some dogs won't ever be totally cool around horse-drawn vehicles. They can learn to be relatively calm, though. Interestingly, a horse-drawn vehicle sets some dogs off more than horses without vehicles. Maybe it is the combination of the clatter of the wheels on the street and the clopping of hooves. Who knows what is going on in those doggie brains?

Naturally there are dogs that remain totally oblivious to the sight and sound of any and all city vehicles. Working with your new puppy or older dog very calmly when you introduce it to the city makes a positive difference. Yelling at your dog when it gets excited about something isn't very productive.

## 5  Treats

You probably have the pattern by now—the last tip is the treat tip. Keep those pockets full of treats to give to your dog whenever goodness prevails. If you don't have clothes with pockets, get a little treat bag to hang on your dog's leash. When your dog is calm around something that has set him off on previous encounters, praise him and give him a treat and a very big hug.

## ~ Seven Tips ~
## Tags, Licenses, And Health And Legal Whatnot

Who wants to pay several hundred dollars for a citation? Who wants to pay several hundred dollars to bail a friend out of jail, especially our best furry friend? Who wants to lose a dog before its time from something that simple shots or paying attention or good control could have prevented? Who wants to have their dog on death row for an issue that training classes or an expert dog behavior specialist could have resolved?

The American Veterinary Medical Association (AVMA) provides a model for city ordinances regarding pets and recommends these dog owner responsibilities:

- All dogs should be kept under restraint.
- No dog should be allowed to cause a nuisance, and the owner should be held responsible.
- Failure to comply with requirements should be subject to fines.
- Dog owners should make sure that their dogs have identification on them at all times that allows determination of the owner.

Because of the professional credibility of the AVMA, most cities take their recommendations seriously. Cities expect dog owners to comply with the rules and regulations the city sets for dogs and their owners.

## 1  Dog License

Most towns and cities have dog license requirements. Each municipality has its own processes and requirements, but most require proof of rabies shots at a minimum. If your city has a website, the requirements are sometimes posted there. Otherwise, you can get the information by calling or stopping by City Hall or the local animal control office. Sometimes a fire station or a police station will be able to give you contact information. In some cases, a fire station will also be able to give you the information you need. Might as well get a license up front and keep it up to date. If you get caught without one, the fine will cost you a whole lot more. Plus, if your dog ever gets lost, the registration tag helps the finder return your dog to you. Enough said about that one.

## 2  Leash Laws

Almost every village, town, suburb, and city has a leash law. That means that Oh-So-Gentle must be leashed at all times when she is not in your home. Of course, there are pet owners who seem to think that rule doesn't apply to their perfect pooch. The second most common complaint I heard about city dogs is that they often run around public spaces off leash. How many times have you heard it? "Oh, she just loves people!" or "Oh, he loves to play with other dogs and he's as gentle as a lamb." or "She's friendly." OK. Right. So what?

Why are there leash laws that force our wonderful friends to be hooked up and kept at our sides when they would love to be romping around and having a doggie blast? Here are a few points to ponder:

- What if you were bitten or threatened by a dog as a child? What if you were out minding your own adult business only to look up to see a dog bouncing around your ankles? I'm sure that would raise some unhappy memories right away. Some parents who were bitten or threatened by dogs teach their children to fear dogs. These children grow up and may teach their children to fear dogs. Fear of dogs is something that can be passed along for generations. Whether this is rational is not up for discussion. It is simply a fact.

- What if you have medical problems with your bones or joints? What if you bruise easily? You would probably cringe in terror at the thought of some fur ball bumping into your legs or, even worse, jumping up on you. Yikes!

- What if that adorable off-leash pooch slobbering all over your politely leashed Poppet is carrying a doggie contagious illness? You could be stuck with a sick dog and vet bills.

- What if your precious little Poppet, off leash, goes dashing around the corner in your apartment building, only to be confronted with a new neighborhood Monster Dog whose owner has no control? Poppet may end up missing a nose (or worse).

- What if you were driving the car that ran over Poppet when she suddenly bounced into the street? How dreadful, especially if you are a dog lover and there was absolutely nothing you could have done to avoid the accident.

- What if you were walking along the sidewalk when the car hit Poppet? Seeing a dog dashing out into a street and getting hit by a car is an awful thing.

- What if Poppet is your dog. Such a horrible loss could have been so easily prevented.

There are so many people and pets out there with so many issues. So many unexpected things could happen. Best to just avoid potentialities and keep Susie Q and Sammy D leashed. Remember, if anything happens to anyone, and your dog is off-leash, your dog is likely to get the blame. As for the accident, even though it is more comfortable to convince yourself that it couldn't happen, the reality is that it *could* happen. An accident is a totally unexpected thing that happens completely out of the blue.

Here are some generic templates for leash laws:

No person shall permit any animal other than a cat to go at large upon any street, public place, or private property other than the property of the owner of the animal. All animals using any street, public place, or private property of anyone other than the owner of the animal shall be on a leash not exceeding six (6) feet in length including the handgrip but excluding the collar and accompanied by a person able to fully control the animal at all times.

No person owning or having possession, charge, custody, or control of any animal shall cause, permit, or allow the animal to stray or in any manner to run at large in or upon any public street, sidewalk, athletic field, athletic facility, or park or upon the property of another, if such animal is not under a physical restraint or a leash so as to allow the animal to be controlled.

All dogs by law are to be under the control of their owner or keeper. Dogs are under control when:
    Confined to the residential property of the owner.
    On a leash no longer than ten feet, controlled by a responsible person.
    In a cage or enclosed interior of a vehicle. It is illegal to transport an unrestrained animal in an open truck bed.

> The leash law is not being followed if Susie Q and Sammy D are wearing leashes and dashing about with their leashes trailing behind them. Compliance means a dog is attached to one end of the leash and a person (not a bicycle) is attached to the other end of the leash. Non-compliance generally means a substantial fine if you are caught.

Every dog needs good healthy exercise, and running around with other dogs is a great way to make this happen. Every dog must be socialized with other dogs. The only way for that to happen is to let dogs run around with other dogs. But not every city has enough places for dogs to run and play. If doggie day care is not for you, and if you don't have a country or suburban place to take your dog for a regular run, you still need to follow the leash laws.

Gather up all the dog owners in town and start lobbying and petitioning your city for more dog runs and more dog parks. Enlist non-dog owners, too. They will be happy to do what is needed to get their parks back and not have to deal with off-leash dogs. Elicit the support of local veterinarians. Work with your local Humane Society for advice on the best way to make your case. Download the American Kennel Club's brochure on establishing a dog park. (At the time of this writing, the link was http://www.akc.org/pdfs/GLEG01.pdf) Don't let your own cynicism block you from taking an active role in improving conditions for your dog. And don't let naysayers try to stop you.

# 3 Shots And Preventive Medications

Make sure your dog is up to date with all its shots and takes all preventive medications on schedule. Proof of some shots is required to obtain a pet license and to take your best friend to training class, dog parks, or doggie day care. If your friend gets sick, be sure to ask the vet whether Pooch can come in contact with other dogs. Some dog diseases are contagious to other dogs. (This is why you don't want your sweet pup to come nose to nose with an unleashed dog, no matter how lovable the unleashed dog may be.)

The AVMA suggests that dogs be given what they call "core" vaccines to protect from diseases that are common to the geographical area. It recommends that you consult with your vet and set up a program that is best for your dog based on its lifestyle, any travel to other areas that you might be planning for your dog, and the contact your dog has with other animals in kennels, obedience classes, and dog parks.

Shots and preventive medications such as heartworm and flea and tick treatments are expensive. They must be given regularly to be effective. Some people don't take that into account when they get a new puppy, so you can't assume that all the dogs your dog may come into contact with are fully vaccinated. Nor should you assume the dogs your dog comes into contact with are receiving preventive medications, or medications for current conditions. This is even more reason for your dog to be fully vaccinated and always up to date. You must include shots and medications not only for the area where you live, but also for any areas where you travel with your dog. Follow the recommendations your vet gives you.

The "quarantine period" required for puppies getting their vaccinations can pose a problem in cities, where your puppy may come into contact with lots of dogs each day. During this time, don't let your puppy play in the dog run or at the dog park. If a doggie day care is willing to accept your puppy before the quarantine period is almost over, it may not be a place you want your dog to attend. When you meet other dogs out on a walk, just pull you pup to the side and explain to the other dog owner that your pup is still in the quarantine period. If possible, take your pup to do its business in places that are not commonly used by other dog owners. I know this is probably next to impossible, but it is best for your puppy if there is any way you can do this. Be observant and see whether you can identify places where not many dog owners take their dogs.

## 4  Dog Boots

Dog boots are not something a human thought up to make dogs more like people. In the Snowbelt, road salt, sidewalk salt, and snow-melting chemicals are harmful to your pet. These are harsh on paw pads and even harsher on tummies when licked off paw pads. Even the "pet-friendly" alternatives are not all that great for your dog. Putting boots on all four paws is time consuming but essential to dog health maintenance if you live in a city.

Initial boot training probably will be a unique experience for both you and your dog. Your dog may exhibit dramatic talents you never would have imagined. In fact, you might want to have the camera handy.

Dude may just stand there in the middle of the room, looking at you in a way he has never looked at you before, convinced that if he stares at you without moving, you will take the things off. Don't take them off. Go read a book or watch the news and let him stand there.

When Dude figures out that the boots are not coming off, he may lift each foot up very, very high one at a time. He may violently shake his paws. He may make himself fall over to make his point. He may howl. He may attack the boots.

Try not to laugh, but if you just can't keep a straight face, leave the room. No matter what, don't take the boots off.

Act Two of the drama comes when there is snow on the ground. Dude refuses to do anything while wearing the boots, but takes care of business just fine when the boots come off. Bundle up, because you may be outside for a while until Dude figures out that this boot thing will happen every time he goes outside in the snow.

It's a good idea to start boot training in the summer so you will have time to practice. Even so, it would be wise to expect a re-enactment of at least some of the drama annually.

The best boots, and naturally the most expensive, are those constructed with leather soles, water-repellant fabric tops, "socks" that come up the leg, and Velcro straps. These offer good protection, stay on well, and can last for several seasons. There are also little rubber boots that look like balloons. This style is good for quick trips out because they are easy to put on, but they don't generally stay on long enough for a long walk or a romp at the dog run.

Whatever type of boots you end up with, you might want to start out with ultra-cheap boots for training (just in case Dude's approach to this ultimate insult is to rip the boots to shreds). When you think you are ready to invest in the real deal, shop around to learn what is out there. Hunting dogs often wear boots, so stores and online sites that cater to hunters are good places to look for high-quality boots. Also check the web for reviews.

If you live in a very hot climate, you might want to look into a type of boot that protects paws from hot sidewalks and streets. Check with your vet about whether their use is recommended for dogs in your area.

## 5  Nipping and Biting

Many of the animal control laws in towns and cities are in place to try to control dog bites and to track dogs that bite. Statistics presented on the website of the

American Veterinary Medical Association are compelling:

- Almost five million people are bitten by dogs every year in the United States.
- Children are the most common victims and are more likely to be injured.
- Most dog bites affecting young children occur during everyday activities and while interacting with familiar dogs.
- Senior citizens are the second most common dog bite victims.

The AVMA offers suggestions to help your dog avoid becoming one of these statistics. Some of those apply to all city dogs:

- Make sure your pet is socialized.
- Don't put your dog in a position where it feels threatened or teased.
- Train your dog.
- Use a leash in public so you have better control over your dog.

Here is the nightmare scenario: Your pet nips or bites someone, you are sued, the dog is quarantined (at best), and life becomes a nightmare. If your dog does bite someone, it will be your fault. No matter what the person did to precipitate the bite, *you* are responsible. Period.

- If your dog does not like to be touched by someone he doesn't know, make sure no one touches him. Only when your dog has made it very clear that a specific person is privileged to pet him is it allowable for that person to pet him. This is OK. A lot of people don't like to be touched by strangers either.

- If your dog is shy, make sure people approach her in whatever manner she requires. Some people are shy, too, so this is understandable.

- If your dog is not accustomed to being around children, *be cautious* about introducing him to a child. Some parents are clueless and want their child to "play with the puppy" no matter how huge and old the dog may be. The child is not usually the problem. Be firm with the child and be even more firm with some parents.

Sometimes you have to be downright rude and ugly to people. Be especially firm with people who are intent on kissing your toy poodle or plunking their two-year-old child down on your Great Dane's back. If they don't pay attention to a polite warning, it is perfectly fine to be rude, ugly, and obnoxious. *Better rude than sued.*

## 6  Tied To The Bicycle Rack And All Alone

How often have you seen a dog outside a shop, attached to a parking meter or lightpost or bicycle rack or table leg? One would hope that "rarely" is the answer to that question, but the answer most people give is "a lot."

Think really hard before attaching your pet to something and popping into a store or other establishment. Even for "just a second," even in the safest of neighborhoods. Granted, it is convenient when you suddenly remember you need to run into the store to pick up something for supper. It is totally inconvenient to have to walk home, drop off the dog, and walk back. And it is so lovely to pop into the coffee shop to pick up a drink, then enjoy it at an outside table at with your dog at your feet.

Most dog owners can come up with an endless list of reasons why it is OK to tie up their dog and just dash inside for a quick minute. The list of reasons *not* to do this is short, but deserves consideration. I'll list three of these reasons.

Good Reason One: It is an invitation to someone to steal your dog. Don't think that your dog can't be stolen, because it can be. As much as you want to believe that your dog won't trot off with just any stranger, you are kidding yourself. Your dog may not trot off with just *any* stranger, but it very well could trot off with someone who somehow convinces it to come along for a walk. Dogs don't have a little conversation with themselves about whether this person will bring them back, or about whether this person is authorized to take them home. They don't listen to the news programs or read the handouts about the risks of going off with strangers.

Good Reason Two: When you are inside, you have no idea if someone is out there taunting our dog or doing something that might make your dog nip or bite. Even if you have the most friendly, people-loving dog in the entire world, people can hurt your dog or tease it to the point that it thinks the behavior must stop. If you are not there to protect your dog, it will probably take it upon itself to do the protecting.

Good Reason Three: Monster Dog may come along. Remember Monster Dog? Monster Dog Owner is seriously out of control of this dog, and your dog may be seriously injured while Monster Dog's Owner stands there in shock.

## 7 Treats

Treat yourself, lavishly and often, if you:

- Keep your dog license up-to-date,
- Follow leash laws,
- Keep your dog current on shots,
- Manage to teach your dog to put up with boots, and
- Are firm when people try to pet your shy dog without permission.

# ~ Eight Tips ~
# Barking

No barking! Period. Dogs that habitually bark are annoying enough when they live a thousand miles from nowhere. In an apartment or condo or city house without acres between you and your neighbor, they are beyond annoying. In many cities, you are breaking a "nuisance" law if you do not control your barking dog.

If nothing in this chapter or in any of the dog training manuals or online resources helps you stop annoyance barking, hire a dog behavior specialist to help you and Loud Mouth figure it out.

OK. That said, let's take a closer look at barking. There are times when barking is appropriate behavior and you want Bruiser to bark. (Yes, I did just contradict myself.) Most of the time, however, Bruiser should not bark.

## 1 Barking Breeds

Some breeds of dogs tend to bark more than other breeds. But there are so-called "quiet breed" dogs that are yappers and there are so-called "barking breed" dogs that are quiet as little mice. The main idea of this section is that dogs can be trained to not bark when barking is not appropriate. Exceptions to this are very, very rare.

If you don't have your dog yet, research various breeds to learn how much they tend to bark. (For that matter, research to discover breeds that you will be able to live with in your urban space. For example, if you love to take long walks, a dog that requires lots of exercise would make a good match for you. But if you are basically a couch potato, you probably would be happier with a couch potato dog breed.)

More than likely you already have your dog, so let's explore barking.

## 2  Learned Barking

Some dogs bark a lot because they were born into a barky family and learned to be noisy when they were puppies. If you visit the breeder a few times and see adult dogs barking for no apparent reason, then you could end up with a pup that barks unnecessarily.

## 3  Rewarded Barking

Sometimes we unwittingly reward barking behavior by paying attention to our dog when it barks. If your dog is warm and dry, doesn't need to go out, doesn't need food or water, and is not in pain, the dog probably shouldn't be barking. If no one is breaking in, your dog probably shouldn't be barking. If you pay attention to the barking, even by yelling, "*Hey. Shut up,*" you reward the barking behavior because you are giving your dog attention.

## 4  Rewarded Silence

Giving dogs lots of attention and treats when they are being quiet rewards quiet behavior. This is not as easy as it sounds. You are busy and your sweet dog has been around for a few years being good and quiet. Sometimes it is really hard to remember to get up and go over to that good, quiet dog to give it a hug and a belly rub.

## 5  Home Alone Barking

Sometimes dogs bark when we are not around. If Angel is usually a perfect little thing, but if your neighbors complain about all her barking, she is barking when you are not around. Neighbors rarely make up this sort of thing. This type of barking can be due to boredom, separation anxiety, or both.

Since you are not around to know whether Angel barks when you are not around, look into any complaints about her barking that you receive. Unfortunately neighbors don't always tell you right to your face. They wait until they are completely frustrated, complain to the other neighbors, then go directly to management or the condo board. It is not a good thing to suddenly show up on management or board radar for a barking dog.

You could install a "puppy cam." You could get a voice-activated recording device. A cheaper way to find out whether or not your dog is a barker is to ask. Visit your neighbors and ask—right side and left side, upstairs and down, and across the hall, too. Don't wait until there are grumbles. Check soon after you move in or get your puppy, and continue to check periodically. Neighbors will appreciate that you are aware that barking is annoying and that you are attempting to prevent it.

If neighbors tell you that they hear barking, assure them that you will begin training right away. If they tell you Angel is barking, but it doesn't bother them, stop the barking anyway. They may change their minds. Check back periodically while you are trying to resolve the issue to see how it is going. Check with them when you think the issue has been resolved, just to be sure. They will appreciate the fact that you are trying to fix the problem, and they will be more likely to go to you instead of management if the barking starts up again.

You can sometimes prevent separation anxiety from developing by not making a big deal out of leaving. Just leave. No big deal. If you will be gone for a while, be sure Angel has food and water and toys. Making sure these things are in place and then doing the actual departure need not be an Academy Award caliber production.

Crate training is another way to prevent separation anxiety from developing. Don't keep Angel in her crate all the time. Do make it a cozy place where she can see the front door, a window, and the TV (if she likes to watch TV). She will more than likely be happy there while you are gone. She may sometimes go into her crate when she wants to block you out. Yes, sometimes dogs want to be alone and not bothered by their humans.

Leaving a television or radio on can help a dog feel less alone. I'm not sure any research has been done to learn the best type of station—classical, jazz, rock, talk, all-day-news, soap operas. Whatever you listen to is what Angel will be accustomed to. If Angel doesn't like your taste, I'm sure she will let you know while you are at home. Change the station and leave something else for her when you are away.

Make sure Angel has safe toys to play with while you are gone. There are dog toys you can stuff with peanut butter or fill with kibble to keep Angel occupied and to stimulate her little brain.

You might want to investigate dog-appeasing pheromone (DAP), available in plug-in diffusers or collars. DAP was developed to calm dogs and reduce stress. People can't smell it, but dogs can. It is pricey, but many people report success with their dogs and DAP. You will find articles about it on the web. Look at multiple sources instead of relying on just one article. The information about DAP indicates that it is safe for dogs and cats, but may not be safe for birds. If Angel is not your only pet, check with your vet before using it.

Doggie day care is a great way for your dog to spend one or more days each week away from home while you are away (or even while you are at home). Angel can play away her energy. She can revel in lots of good dog socialization. She can enjoy tons of attention and petting and hugs.

Having a dog walker come once or twice a day is another wonderful thing for Angel. She can get a little exercise, and having someone to play with breaks the monotony of being alone all day. It reduces the potential for accidents.

Some people get another dog for their Angel to play with. Sometimes that works, but sometimes it raises other issues. If you choose this option, you then have two dogs to deal with in the city. Ponder this idea very carefully before you add a second dog to your home. Get thoughts and opinions from your vet, dog trainer, friends, and online resources before taking this step. If, after much research and deliberation, you decide a second dog is the answer, then you and Angel need to find the right dog friend for her.

## 6  Normal Barking

Sometimes barking can be OK. When a dog barks because he has something to say, he will probably not go on and on and on and on ...

- He may bark while he is standing by his food or water dish. "Hellooooo—I need your help here!"

- He may bark when he needs to go out and you have ignored all prior signals. "Wake up Person-Pet. Pay attention. I cannot wait much longer. Don't you see that my back legs are crossed and I am trying to hold it?????"

- He may bark when he is playing with his toys. "This is soooooooo much fun!"

- He may bark when he hears someone near the door. "Hey, you. I mean you. I hope you have good business being near my door. If not you had best skedaddle right now."

> Normal barking becomes nuisance barking when your dog barks every time he hears the neighbors come down the hall and go into their next-door or across-the-hall homes.

- He may bark if someone breaks in. You hope he would bark if someone breaks in. "If you come one step farther into this space, you will not have a leg to stand on. See my sharp teeth? Get Out Now!"

## 7  Two More Tips

Giving Yipper something to do when he launches into a barking jag is a good way to stop the barking. *Yipper, sit!* or *Yipper, down!* will get his attention and give him something else to do. If you teach him tricks, you will be able to redirect his behavior. *Yipper, fetch your ball!* or *Yipper, say your prayers!* (Even if your dog isn't a barker, teaching him tricks is a great way for you to bond.)

Yipper should also be taught a command to help him stop barking. As you do with the other commands, say *Hush!* or *Quiet!* or whatever word you choose in a commanding voice. Don't use a yelling voice. Yipper will think you are barking back if you yell at him. Then he will bark back at you and you will yell at him and he will bark back...it doesn't solve the problem. When Yipper stops barking on command, praise him and give him a treat.

Sometimes you might need to physically stop his barking. Do not hit Yipper. He is just being a dog. Try a gentle correction technique Yipper's mother used with her puppies when they became annoying. Place one of your hands over his nose—place, don't squeeze. Place your other hand on the back of his neck behind his ears. Don't squeeze. As you place your hands on him, give him the no-bark command once. Hold him for just a second after the barking stops and then remove your hands and use them to give Yipper a hug and a treat. If you use this technique, do not leap toward Yipper and frighten him. Do not squeeze his nose or his neck and hurt him. Don't yell the command. This is not meant to be a punishment. You are holding him as a gentle reminder that he must settle down. I will say right here that there are some trainers who do not like this technique; there are others who teach it. It is an option for you to try, or for you to talk about with your trainer.

## 8  Resources

If you have a new puppy, work with it to prevent nuisance barking from the start. If you have a nuisance barker, please seek help.

There are Internet resources. There are books devoted to teaching dogs not to bark and helping dogs stop nuisance barking. There are dog trainers and dog behavior experts who can work with you and your dog. If training is not working, your trainer may recommend the use of a no-bark collar. These collars emit a high-pitched sound or a spray or even a shock when a dog barks. No-bark collars are to be used as a last resort, not first resort. You might want to check with your vet before taking this step.

The topic of nuisance barking is much too complex to cover in detail in this small book, but it must be addressed. Nuisance barking annoys neighbors. It can get you evicted. It could be signaling a more serious problem with your dog. In cities with laws that mandate that dog owners keep barking under control, it could become expensive in terms of fines.

# ~ Eleven Tips ~
# Miscellaneous This And That

There are many things to think about when you step out of the door and into the city with your dog. Two important things are:

- Always be alert; pay attention to your dog and your surroundings
- Always be prepared—for anything.

Even more important is to not let yourself feel overwhelmed. Reading all these do's and don'ts can make the whole thing seem daunting. But most of these tips are just common sense. They will become habit in no time, and make every trip outside with your dog easy and fun.

## 1  Treats

In this chapter, treats come first. Be sure you always have yummy treats with you—to reward your dog when he's good, to bribe your dog when he's thinking about doing something he shouldn't, to give to other people to give to your dog, and to give to dogs you meet along the way. If you are walking your dog enough, and if you are using small, healthy treats, there is no need to worry about your dog becoming fat on rewards.

Some trainers do not advocate the use of treats for training and rewards. You can probably guess that I am not in that camp. However, I do believe that hugs and good belly rubs and back rubs are very, very effective. Treats are in addition to these rewards and should not take their place. But out and about in the city, you can't beat treats for convenience when a quick special reward is in order after a "city situation" has been successfully averted or navigated.

> Don't forget to take the treats out of your pocket when you finish training or return home. Otherwise, if Bingo is your typically smart dog, you may find holes in your pockets where he has scarfed up the leftovers.

A last word on treats: Don't ever forget to reward yourself for having a wonderful, well-mannered dog. Every time your dog receives a complement for being good, remember that your patience and diligence is the reason. Give yourself a wonderful treat.

## 2 Lost Dogs

Your dog may get lost. Sometimes stuff happens in spite of all our best efforts.

This is not the time to panic or weep. Save that for later, when your dog is safely home.

I hope you have already scratched your current cell phone number on your dog's tag. (Your dog *is* wearing her tag, isn't she?) And I hope you have had your dog tattooed or had a chip inserted for just such an emergency.

Regardless of whether your dog has identifying information, when you have looked around and realized that it is missing, take the following steps *immediately*. Right away. Not a moment to lose.

1. Contact your local animal control organization, the fire station, any company or city department that may have workers in the area. Contact the police, but *do not* call 911. This is not a 911 emergency no matter how much you love your dog. Contact your local animal shelter, the Humane Society, and local animal rescue groups. Contact vets and emergency pet clinics in the area where the dog got lost. It is possible that not all of these organizations will be sympathetic when you call, but just thank them for their help anyway. Now they know about your dog and someone will keep an eye out—even if they sounded annoyed that you called them, and told you that your lost dog was not their responsibility.

2. Walk around telling everyone you see. *Everyone.* Someone may have seen your dog trotting off after something interesting.

3. Call for your dog and wave treats around in the air (you *always* have treats with you). Do this even if you appear insane to all around. Dogs can hear and smell from a long way off. They recognize familiar sounds and smells and will come toward them.

4. If you are in an area familiar to your dog, go home after checking around. Your dog may be waiting at the door wondering what took you so long.

5. Make notices with your pet's identifying features, a picture if you have one, and a contact number. *Don't* include your name or address, for your own safety. If you can afford it, state "Reward will be given," but don't say how much. Post the notices on streetlights. Post them in neighborhood stores, pubs, cafes, salons, tattoo parlors—any business in your neighborhood that is willing to let you post a flyer or leave some for customers to pick up. Hand them out everywhere you go. Post them in nearby apartments and condos. Put them on front doors of neighborhood homes. Post online if there is a pet lost-and-found website for your area.

When your dog gets home, call everyone you previously contacted to let them know they can stop looking. Remove all the notices you posted so they won't be littering the neighborhood with out-of-date information. Now you can panic and cry and do whatever you wanted to do when you discovered your dog was lost. Reward yourself for doing sensible things instead.

> 1. Be careful of scammers who try to claim the reward.
> 2. If someone calls about having found your pet, arrange to meet in a public place during the day, for your safety.
> 3. If you give a reward, give cash, not a check (to keep your banking information private).

## 3 Wet Dog

It is a good idea to have a rug just inside your door (and another one outside your door if your building allows). This provides one or two places for little paws to deposit mud before they reach your carpet. Keep a towel by the door during your rainy and snowy seasons and give your dog a good rubdown before he gets everything wet. (He probably will have already done his great shake in the lobby or in the elevator—wherever there were the largest number of people for him to get all wet.)

If Sphinx is into tricks, two tricks are very useful here. These are *Shake!* and *High Five!* If your giant dog will obey these two commands, it is much easier to get those paws up off the floor. It will be easier for you to wipe the mud off, to put the snow boots on, and to take the snow boots off. If you have a tiny dog you can pick up, these tricks are cute but not quite as useful.

## 4  Elevators

In some buildings, dogs are not allowed in elevators. Some cities have ordinances prohibiting dogs in elevators. Be sure to check into this if you are looking at condos and apartments on an upper floor. You may not want to add hiking up and down stairs to your exercise routine.

Other buildings require you to take a service elevator with your dog. Sometimes this rule is not enforced until someone complains to management or to the condo board, causing a major crackdown. Might as well stick to the rule and not be the cause for the lowering of the boom.

If you are allowed to take your dog in the regular passenger elevator, please be aware that others in the elevator may be afraid of dogs or may be allergic to dog dander. Not many dog owners think about asking people who are already in the elevator whether they would mind if a dog joined them, but that is a very thoughtful thing to do.

Who knows what goes through doggie brains when confronted with the elevator experience. If you live on an upper floor, Floppy will have to learn to deal with elevators; the sooner you start, the better. Don't be tempted to carry Floppy into the elevator when she is a puppy if she will grow up to be a large dog.

- Some dogs cower in a corner and don't want anyone to come near them when they are in an elevator.
- Other dogs act as they act in any other room.
- Some dogs are perfectly fine in an elevator that carries only the two of you in it, but go into protective mode when other people are in the elevator. This is a tiny space, and some dogs don't feel comfortable when other people or dogs are crammed up against their person-pet.
- Other dogs are fine sharing an elevator with other people, but turn into Elevator Monster Dog if they have to share with another dog.

Until you have had a variety of elevator experiences repeatedly, don't assume that your dog will have the same personality in an elevator that it has outside one.

Four serious safety rules pertain to dogs and elevators:

1. Don't barge into an elevator without looking to see whether someone is getting off. Stand to the side and allow people to get off without having to worry about your dog.

2. Don't barge onto an elevator without looking to see whether there is another dog in the elevator, or if children are in the elevator. Pay attention—elevators are full of disaster potential.

3. Hang on to your dog's leash and keep your dog close to you. If you use a retractable leash, it should be retracted all the way and locked in that position.

4. Keep your dog close to you when getting on and off the elevator. The last thing you want is for the elevator door to close with you on one side and your dog on the other.

## 5  Crates

Most apartments and some condos will require your dog to be crated when maintenance is done in your unit. Even if you don't use a crate for any other reason, you will probably need to have one and you should accustom your dog to being in it. If you are moving your dog to a city from the country or a suburb and your dog has never been in a crate, start crate training before you move, if possible. Dog training books and online resources are excellent sources of instruction for selecting the right type of crate and for crate training, so we will leave it at that.

## 6  Fireworks

Fireworks are part of summer weekend life in some cities. Some dogs that are completely uninterested in fireworks. Others go into major panic mode. Dog training resources online have good advice about how to handle fireworks. Some recommend crating, if your dog is calm, cozy, and happy in a crate. DAP is another solution (discussed in the Barking section.) If none of the suggestions you find online seem to work for your Nelly, and if DAP is not a good solution for Nelly, discuss the situation with your vet. A mild sedative may be prescribed for her if your vet thinks that is the best approach.

## 7  Fire Alarms

If you live in a multi-story building, there will be times when the fire alarms go off. Fire alarms are painful to our ears, so you can imagine how they affect the sound-sensitive ears of a dog. Even the calmest of dogs may go bonkers at the sound of fire alarms.

Fire drills and fire alarm tests present one fire alarm situation. Insist that the management let you know in advance exactly when the alarm testing will occur, so you can get your dog out of the building. If you will be at home or if your dog is scheduled for doggie day care that day, great. But that isn't always the way luck would have it. See whether your dog can stay with a friend for the day, or add a day to the doggie day care schedule. If a full day away is not feasible, see whether you can pin management down as to the time of the alarm test or drill, then schedule your dog walker to have the dog out of the building at that time. If you learn that there was a test and your management did not inform you ahead of time, become a squeaky wheel so it doesn't happen again. This is the easy fire alarm situation.

It there is a fire when you are not home, it could become a tragedy. When you move in or when you get your dog, learn the management policy for notifying the fire department about units that contain animals. Ask management where your dog will be taken if it is removed from the building, so you won't have to find that information in a panic situation. It is a good idea to attach a decal to at least one exterior window and to the door, indicating that there is an animal inside the unit. These decals are available at some fire stations and some pet stores. They are also available online.

A bad (but not awful) situation is when there is an unannounced fire drill, alarm test, or false alarm, and you are not there. You may return home some day to find your dog is behaving strangely—hiding under something, acting like Velcro-pet, howling…any number of completely unusual behaviors. It could be that the fire alarms went off that day. There is nothing you can do at this time, but be extra nice to your poor dog for the rest of the evening. Contact your management to be sure that you are notified of all future testing and drills. False alarms are out of everyone's control.

The fourth situation is when the fire alarms go off, unannounced, and you are there. You cannot know whether it is the real thing, an unannounced drill, or a false alarm. It doesn't matter. You must leave the building immediately.

> - Do not let the dog out of your unit until his leash is firmly attached to his collar on one end and to your hand on the other end.
> - Do not use a retractable leash.
> - Even if your dog is small enough to carry, you must still attach him to a leash.

The fire fighters will not think any dog is cute in the middle of a fire. Your neighbors will not think your dog is cute in this particular situation. This is pure business. In the middle of all the noise and all the people, you must keep your dog under total and complete control, right up next to you, and focused on going down the stairs in pace with everyone else.

If you live in a typical downtown apartment building, there will probably be lots of false alarms. They generally happen in the middle of the night in a storm. For your own safety, you must grab your dog, head out, and keep going until you hear it's safe to go back. Your dog may get used to the experience, but probably won't get used to the noise.

## 8  Wheelchairs

Approach wheelchairs with caution until you are sure your dog is OK with them. Some dogs are fine, other dogs are spooked by thme. Unless the occupant specifically invites such behavior, your dog should not put its paws or its entire self into the person's lap. Never, ever.

## 9  Outdoor Events

Celebrations, street fairs, concerts, and open-air markets are a part of summer in the city. They are a wonderful conglomeration of the things this book talks about.

> Some outdoor events do not allow pets. If pets are not allowed, that means your dog, too. *Really.* It does.

Many outdoor events welcome dogs. Give serious thought to taking your dog to an event. Do a reality check about your dog's personality and take a realistic view of what the event will be like. Don't be in denial:

- Your dog may get hurt.
- Your dog may hurt someone.
- Your dog may become stressed.
- Events often have a large share of pickled people (remember that section).

You might love having your dog with you, but your dog might prefer being cozy at home and might be safer there, too.

If you do decide to take your dog to an event:

- If you have a tiny dog, keep TaterTott off the ground. In a crowd, people won't be aware of little dogs. People who take babies to events keep them in arms, or in strollers that are annoyingly in the way, to keep people from stepping on them. Use that as a model. Keep TaterTott up off the ground, in your arms or in your bag, out of the way of big feet with shoes on them.

- If Sassy is a larger dog, keep her glued to your side. It keeps her out of the way of other people. It also prevents people from getting tangled in the leash between you and Sassy. Most people will be absorbed in themselves and their friends, and won't be paying attention to anything else, including a leash.

- If the crowd is large, it is probably not the place for your dog to romp with his buddy Pete when they run into each other. The two dogs are, of course, on their leashes. Not only will the dogs be tangling up in their leashes, the unobservant can get tangled up, too. And the dogs could crash into passersby; they definitely won't be paying attention to the people, nor will the dogs care. But the people will definitely care. You and Pete's owner will probably be chatting and not paying close enough attention. Save the romp with Pete for another time and place.

Even though it is absolutely appropriate for you to take your dog and you are sure your dog will enjoy the event, you might feel a bit intimidated the first time you venture into an event with your furry friend. But if Tubs is an event kind of dog, he will love it. There is so much to smell and so much to see. That little doggie brain will be in full gear the whole time you are there. Of course Tubs will be on best behavior and win lots of treats from vendors, performers, and others who keep treats to give to good dogs.

## 10  My Dog is Friendly

This has been discussed several times in this book, but it is important enough to have its own section. How many times have you heard people who are with their dog (on and off a leash) say, "He's friendly" or "He loves people" or "He loves other dogs"? Probably more often than you can count. This is totally beside the point in practically every city situation. It is irrelevant. It doesn't make any sense. It is equivalent to walking up to a complete stranger and saying, "Peanuts are growing in Africa." The only time it applies to anything at all is when someone comes up and asks you whether your dog is friendly, or asks whether your dog loves people, or asks if your dog loves other dogs. In every other case, it doesn't matter how friendly your dog is. The other dog may not be. The person your dog runs up to may have a serious issue with dogs. The dog your dog happily bounces up to greet may have a contagious disease. It is *not* about friendly. It is about safety.

## 11  Walking More Than One Dog

If you take more than one dog out at the same time, then each of the tips in this book applies individually to each of the dogs in your pack. Each dog will have its own personality. Each may react differently to the same situation. Each may have its own learning style when you are training. Each may have its own treat preferences. Double diligence. Triple diligence. Diligence for each dog.

If one or more of the dogs in your pack is Monster Dog, then MD should be walked solo until all issues are resolved.

# Some Last Words

Just a few more things, and you and your dog will be well on your way to living and loving life in the city together.

## 1 Training

It cannot be said too often that this book should not replace standard dog training manuals and dog training classes. This is a survival guide, a supplement, a book of tips to bridge the gap between traditional dog training rules and the realities of city life. Because of the unique demands of city life, some of the traditional dog training rules vary:

- Some may be of even greater importance in urban environments because they are needed more often than in suburbia or in the country (such as "*Leave it*" and "*Drop it*").
- Some need slight modifications (such as training your dog to walk on both sides of you, and knowing you *can* housebreak your dog anywhere— even in a noisy, crowded place)
- Some are applied under new conditions (such as remaining calm in an elevator and keeping dog noses out of plates in sidewalk cafes).

If you are moving your dog into a city from the suburbs or the country, enrolling your dog in a training class will help her learn to adjust to other dogs. You can do this before you move, as a transition. You can do this after you move, to introduce her to some neighborhood dogs. You can do this both before and after you move, because it is really hard to participate in too many training classes.

## 2  Dogs In The City

In the past, many people believed that dogs are for suburban or country living only and that they don't belong in a city. Some still hold this opinion. But the truth is, many dogs take to urban living without any problems at all. City dwellers are beginning to insist on being able to have dogs. People migrating into the cities are demanding that they be allowed to bring their dogs with them. As a result, more and more urban living spaces are beginning to welcome our pets.

This is relatively new in many cities, though, and things could quickly revert to the "No Dogs Allowed" days. Conversations with apartment owners and condo board members who have moved back to a "No Dogs" policy have given me insight into what it is that makes people back off decisions to allow dogs. Conversations with people who don't like dogs have given me insight into why our best friends are so unpopular with some people. And observations of too many dog owners have confirmed many of the complaints I've heard in these conversations.

It is up to each of us to make sure our pets are well mannered. First, because it is so much easier to live with a well-mannered pet. Second, because it is much nicer for our neighbors if we have well-mannered pets. And finally, if for no other reason, because having well-mannered pets goes a long way to assuring that the privileges of having our dogs with us is not taken away.

Dog owners are going through a trial period and we want to make sure that the privilege of having our dogs turns into a right. To do that, we need to honor our responsibilities. "Dog Friendly" does not mean our dogs can romp around out of control. "Dog Friendly" does mean that people are friendly to the notion of having dogs around.

Even though I have heard about and seen more bad examples than I would like, I have also heard about and seen more good than bad. I think we are trending in the right direction.

## 3  Take-Aways

Dog training tips for city living in summary:

- High-rise housebreaking is not as hard as it might seem, but it does require some creative adjustments to the traditional rules.
- Cities are full of an assortment of people and animals. Some of them will present challenges.
- Every city dog *must* know some essential commands.

- Health and legal matters need to be attended to.
- City living presents unique opportunities, unique situations, and unique circumstances that require special dog manners.
- There are some things that some people don't like about some people's dogs. Three very specific complaints are at the top of the list of most city people, including many city dog owners:
  - The dogs have owners who don't pick up after them.
  - The dogs have owners who let them run around off-leash in public spaces.
  - The dogs have owners who don't stop nuisance barking.

Another way to sum up the tips in this book are these three commitments that we can make to our city dogs:

- Your life is in my hands. I will do what is required to keep you safe and healthy.
- I will make sure that you and I stay out of trouble by being legal and following the laws of our city.
- I will be mindful of the people who share our living space and our play space, so people will have only good things to say about you.

# 4  Have Fun

Have fun with your city dog. Teach your best furry friends good manners and lots of tricks. City dogs have a great deal of fun and get an incredible amount of attention. They get to go on walks several times every single day. They get to meet lots of people and other critters they would never get to meet if they didn't live in the city. If they like to be petted, there are so many people who love to pet them. They get to smell an unbelievable amount of new smells every time they go outside. Plus, if they are the social type, they are right on hand for parades and street fairs and festivals. With a dog, just going on a walk around a city block can be an adventure.

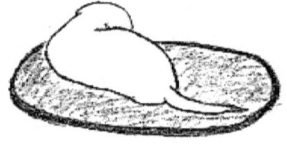

# Index

**A**
American Veterinary Medical Association (AVMA), 74

**B**
bad things for dogs to eat, 49
barking, 43, 88–96
barking breeds, 88–89
barking, more tips to prevent, 95
bell ringing, 24–26
bicycles, 71–72
biting, 83–85
boots for dogs, 81–83
busses, 72

**C**
carpets, 27–28
cats, 45
children, 37–38
chipmunks, 44–45
choke chain collars, 64
city ordinances, 74–75
cleaning up after your dog, 28–30
collars and leashes, 64–65
*Come!* command, 49, 62–64
commands, 48–66
commitments to pets, 115
common complaints, 115
core vaccines, 80
crate training, 92
crates, 104–105
cue words, 22–24

**D**
DAP (dog appeasing pheromone), 92–93, 105
diseases, 46, 76–77, 80
distraction, dealing with, 22–24
dog boots, 81–83
dog dislikers, 32–33
dog licenses, 75
dog lovers, 33–34, 36
dog parks and dog runs, 63–64, 79
dog security, 86
dog walkers, 93
doggie day care, 81, 93
Double-loop leashes, 64–65
*Down and stay!* command, 62–64
*Down!* command, 49, 63
*Drop it!* command, 49, 54–57
drunks, 34–35

**E**
elevators, 102–104
essential commands, 48–66
exercise, 79

**F**
fear factor, 19–22
fear of dogs, 41, 76
fines, 36, 75, 79, 96
fire alarms, 105–107
fireworks, 105
flea and tick treatments, 80
flowers and plants, 69–70
food stores, 69

**G**
geese, 44–45
guide dogs, 42–43

**H**
harness collars, 64
head collars, 64, 65
heartworm medication, 80
*Heel quick! / Heel slow!,* 61
*Heel right! / Heel left!,* 58
*Heel!* command, 49, 57–61
*High Five!* trick, 102
home alone barking, 90–93
horses, 43–44, 72
housebreaking, 19–31
Humane Society, 41, 48, 79, 99
*Hurry up!* cue word, 23, 61
*Hush!* command, 95

**I**
identification, 100
inline skates, 71
inside-outside doors, 24–25

**K**
keys, 26–27

**L**
learned barking, 89

leash bags, 29
leash laws, 75–79
leashes, 64–65
*Leave it!* command, 49, 51–54
licenses, dog, 75
litter boxes for dogs, 21–22
long leads, 63
lost dogs, 98–101

**M**
mail carriers, 36
monkeys, 45
Monster Dog, 39–41, 87

**N**
Nature's Miracle (spot cleaner), 28
neighbor relations, 91, 104
nipping and biting, 83–85
no-bark collars, 96
non-dog pets, 45–47
normal barking, 94
nuisance barking, 94, 96

**O**
obedience commands, 48–66
*Off!* command, 63
outdoor events, 108–110
outdoor markets, 69
overly friendly dogs, 41–42

**P**
paper training, 21–22
park etiquette, 44
patience, 50
peer pressure, 29
people, dogs and, 32–38
petiquette, 15

physical correction techniques, 95–96
picking up after your dog, 28–30
pickled people, 34–35
plants and flowers, 69–70
play, 66
police officers, 36
poo bags, 29
pot-belly pigs, 45
practice, 49–50
preventive medications, 80–81
prong collars, 64
puppy classes, 48–49

**Q**
quarantine period for puppies, 81
*Quiet!* command, 95

**R**
retractable leashes, 65, 104, 107
rewarded barking, 89–90
rewarded silence, 90
rewards for lost dogs, 100, 101
roller skates, 71

**S**
separation anxiety, 91–92
service dogs, 42–43
*Shake!* trick, 102
shots, 80–81
sidewalk cafes, 67–68
*Sit!* command, 49
skateboards, 70
spot shampooers, 27
squirrels, 44–45

*Stay!* command, 49
stores, 68–69
Surprise Monster Dog, 40

**T**
theft, dog, 86
training classes, 16–17, 48, 112–113
treats (for dogs), 30–31, 38, 47, 66, 73, 97–98
treats (for dog owners), 87, 98
tricks, 35, 102
tricks classes, 17
trolleys and trucks, 72

**U**
unattended dogs, 85–87
uniforms, people in, 35–36

**V**
vaccines, 80–81
vehicles, 70–73

**W**
walk the other way, 42, 46, 60
walking more than one dog, 111
wet dog, 101–102
wheelchairs, 108

**Y**
yelling, 50, 59, 73, 90, 95, 96

# Dog Topics You Might Want To Internet Search For More Detail

Barking Control

Bell Training A Dog

Bow Command

Chain Collar

Come Command

Crate Training

DAP

Dog Aggression, Aggressive Dogs

Dog Boots

Dog Harness Collar

Dog Head Collar

Dog Parks And Dog Runs In Your Area

Dog Trainers And Training Facilities In Your Area

Dogs And Children

Double Loop Leash

Down Command

Drop It Command

Exercising Your Dog
Fire Safety Tips For Dogs
Getting A Second Dog
Healthy Dog Treats
High Five Command
Heel Command
Housebreaking Cue Words
Housebreaking Methods
Leash Laws For Your Area
Leave It Command
Licensing Requirements For Your Area
Litter Boxes For Dogs
Lost Dog Locater Services In Your Area
No-Bark Collars
Pet Emergency Clinics In Your Area
Plants Dangerous To Dogs
Prong Collar
Separation Anxiety In Dogs
Shake Command
Sit Command
Stay Command
Training Methods For Dogs

Katherine Kane, an urban dog owner with over 30 years experience working with dogs, has based this book on her experience and on conversations with city dog owners, apartment and condo management, animal control and Humane Society personnel, urban vets, dog trainers, and people who object to dogs being anywhere in cities.

Katherine's next book, scheduled for publication in 2011, will give dog owners tips on keeping their dogs safe, healthy, and happy.

# Bonus Pages

# One Section From The Next Book

# Foods Your Dog Should Avoid

Starting on the next page is a list of foods common in our kitchens that are dangerous to dogs, and other foods we should be careful about giving to our dogs.

There professional and annecdotal disagreement about the safety of some of the foods listed here. Some vets will say, "No way!"; others will say "No problem" about the same food. Some people say that their dog has eaten something without any problems; other people tell horror stories about one of their dogs eating the same thing. Dogs, like people, have different tolerance levels. Some foods that might cause reactions in one dog may not have the same effect on another dog.

But there is no disagreement about the danger of your dog eating some of the foods on this list. If your dog eats any of the foods listed here that are not highly toxic, keep your eye on it for a day or two in case there is a reaction. If your dog eats any of the more toxic foods, contact your vet or local pet emergency clinic immediately.

> It is important to do your own research and talk with your vet before making a decision to feed your dog any "people food".

| | |
|---|---|
| **Alcoholic Beverages** | can cause vomiting, diarrhea, lack of coordination, central nervous system problems, tremors, difficulty breathing, metabolic imbalances, coma, or death—the smaller the dog, the more danger alcoholic beverages present |
| **Artificial Sweeteners that contain Xylitol** | Xylitol can can cause a sudden drop in blood sugar, resulting in depression, loss of coordination and seizures; it can also cause liver failure |
| **Avocados** | some sources state that avocados can cause heart and breathing problems, in addition to diarrhea and vomiting if a large amount is eaten |

| | |
|---|---|
| **Bacon** and **Bacon Grease** | because of the high fat content, bacon can lead to vomiting, diarrhea, and if given often, even pancreatitis |
| **Baking Powder** and **Baking Soda** | Baking powder can cause electrolyte changes, muscle spasms and congestive heart failure.<br><br>Some resources recommend using baking soda for brushing a pet's teeth and for litter box odor control. However, other resources warn that in a large amount, it can have the same effect as baking powder. |
| **Bologna** | contains lots of sodium nitrates, and fat, so they are not a good nutritional choice |

| | |
|---|---|
| **Bones** | There is quite a bit of disagreement about whether or not dogs should eat bones of any type. They have been known to cause injuries in the mouth, choking, blockage, and laceration of organs. Do some research and ask your vet about giving your dog bones. |
| **Broccoli** | can be toxic to dogs if eaten in large amounts; although some people recommend small amounts as healthy for dogs |
| **Caffeine** | is toxic and can affect the heart and nervous systems |
| **Cat Food** | is not good for dogs because it is too high in protein and fats |

| | |
|---|---|
| **Chocolate** | can cause vomiting, diarrhea, hyperactivity, panting, abnormal heart rhythm, tremors, seizures, and even death (the darker the chocolate, the more toxic it is to dogs) |
| | NOTE: If you use cocoa mulch in your garden, it is a byproduct of chocolate and can cause the same problems. Probably not in your kitchen, but I thought I would just toss this bit of information into the chart anyway. |
| **Citrus Peels** and **Citrus Oil Extracts** | can cause vomiting, and have been linked to irritation and possibly even central nervous system depression if eaten in a large quantity |
| **Coffee** | like all other food or drink with caffeine, can be toxic and affect the heart and nervous systems; it can also cause vomiting |

| | |
|---|---|
| **Corn Cob** | will not digest and may need to be surgically removed |
| **Dairy Products** | are not very dangerous, but can result in diarrhea in some adult dogs (most dogs can tolerate a small amount of yogurt and cheese) |
| **Diet Products that contain Xylitol** | Xylitol can can cause a sudden drop in blood sugar, resulting in depression, loss of coordination and seizures; it can also cause liver failure. |
| **Eggs–raw** | can lead to skin and hair coat problems; they may also contain salmonella, which is as harmful to pets as it is to humans |
| **Fat Trimmings** | a large amount of fat in a regular basis is not good for dogs, and can cause pancreatitis over time |

| | |
|---|---|
| **Fish—raw** | if eaten regularly and often, can lead to loss of appetite, seizures, and in severe cases, death; there have been reported issues with dogs frequently eating raw salmon |
| **Garlic— raw, cooked, powder** | eaten in large amounts, can cause unusual changes in a dog's red blood cells and cause anemia, so if you spill a jar of garlic powder or a handful of garlic cloves, clean it up before your dog gets into it |
| **Grapes** | contain a toxin that can cause kidney failure if eaten in large quantities |
| **Liver** | more than a couple of times a week, over time, can cause deformed bones, excessive bone growth on the elbows and spine, weight loss, and anorexia |

| | |
|---|---|
| **Macadamia Nuts** | can cause weakness, muscle tremor and paralysis (symptoms are usually temporary) |
| **Mushrooms** | even if they are safe for humans, may affect multiple systems in a dog's body, causing shock, and possibly death |
| **Nutmeg** | can cause tremors, seizures and death |
| **Onions—raw, cooked, powder** | contain sulfoxides and disulfides, which can damage red blood cells and cause anemia (chives, shallots, and leeks should also be avoided) |
| **Peppers** | hot peppers contain capsaicin, which can irritate a dog's skin, nose, eyes, and gastrointestinal system (bell peppers can be eaten in moderation by many dogs) |

| | |
|---|---|
| **Pharmaceutical Products For Humans**—prescription, over-the-counter, and off-the-shelf | can result in any number of problems for dogs, and should not be given without the express permission of your vet |
| **Pits** and **Seeds** from apples, apricots, cherries, peaches, pears, plums | can cause obstruction of the digestive tract; some of these seeds and pits can cause exposure to cyanide |
| **Popcorn** | can pose a choking hazard, and the hulls and seeds are not digestible |

| | |
|---|---|
| **Potato Leaves, Potato Stems,** and **Raw Potatoes** | contain solanine, which affects the digestive, nervous, and urinary systems, resulting in a wide range of symptoms like drooling, vomiting and diarrhea, loss of appetite, drowsiness, central nervous system depression, confusion, dilated pupils, and slowed heart rate |
| **Processed Lunchmeats** | contain lots of sodium nitrates, and fat, so they are not a good nutritional choice for a dog |
| **Raisins** | contain a toxin that can cause kidney failure if eaten in large quantities |
| **Rhubarb** | cooked should not be a problem in small quantities; but the leaves are very toxic to dogs and can affect the digestive, nervous, and urinary systems |

| | |
|---|---|
| **Salt** in large quantities | may lead to electrolyte imbalances |
| **Sausage Grease** | like bacon grease, is not good for your dog and in large amounts can lead to vomiting, diarrhea, and even pancreatitis |
| **Seeds and pits** from apples, apricots, cherries, peaches, pears, plums | can cause obstruction of the digestive tract; some of these seeds and pits can cause exposure to cyanide |

| | |
|---|---|
| **Sodas** | like all other food or drink with caffeine, can be toxic and affect the heart and nervous systems; it can also cause vomiting |
| | NOTE: "sugar-free" sodas may also contain Xylitol. This substance can cause a sudden drop in blood sugar, resulting in depression, loss of coordination and seizures; it can also cause liver failure. |
| **Tea** | like all other food or drink with caffeine, can be toxic and affect the heart and nervous systems; it can also cause vomiting |
| **Tobacco** | affects the digestive and nervous systems, and can result in rapid heart beat, collapse, coma, and death |

| | |
|---|---|
| **Tomato leaves and stems** | contain solanine, which affects the digestive, nervous, and urinary systems, resulting in a wide range of symptoms like drooling, vomiting and diarrhea, loss of appetite, drowsiness, central nervous system depression, confusion, dilated pupils, and slowed heart rate |
| **Uncooked meat** | may cause E. coli or Salmonella |
| **Vitimin Supplements For Humans** | the iron in vitamin supplements can damage the lining of the digestive system and be toxic to ther organs including the liver and kidneys |

| | |
|---|---|
| **Walnuts** | can cause an upset stomach and diarrhea. If the walnuts have fungus or mold (generally if picked up outside), they can cause vomiting, trembling, drooling, lack of coordination, lethargy, loss of appetite, and jaundice. Severely affected dogs can produce blood-tinged vomit or stools. Dogs can take several days to exhibit serious signs of illness. |
| **Xylitol** in **Diet products** and **Artificial sweeteners** | Xylitol can can can cause a sudden drop in blood sugar, resulting in depression, loss of coordination and seizures; it can also cause liver failure |
| **Yeast dough** | can expand and produce gas in the digestive system, causing pain and possible rupture of the stomach or intestines |

www.ingramcontent.com/pod-product-compliance
Lightning Source LLC
Chambersburg PA
CBHW071702040426
42446CB00011B/1880